Dear
CISGENDER
People

Kenny
Ethan
Jones

Dear CISGENDER People

A Guide to Trans Allyship and Empathy

*To the bestest ally in the world,
my mum, Edwina Mary Jones.*

*When I wasn't strong enough to fight on my
own, she fought for me. When I felt heartbroken
by the way the world treated me, she loved me
extra hard. Her love gave me the strength to
become the man I am today.*

Acquisitions Editor Marleigh Price
Project Editor Izzy Holton
Senior Production Editor David Almond
Production Controller Kariss Ainsworth
Art Director Maxine Pedliham
Editorial Director Elizabeth Neep
Publishing Director Katie Cowan

Jacket Designer Anna Morrison & Maxine Pedliham
Cover photograph Kiran Gidda

First published in Great Britain in 2024 by
Dorling Kindersley Limited
DK, One Embassy Gardens, 8 Viaduct Gardens,
London, SW11 7BW

The authorised representative in the EEA is
Dorling Kindersley Verlag GmbH. Arnulfstr. 124,
80636 Munich, Germany

A CIP catalogue record for this book
is available from the British Library.
ISBN: 978-0-2415-8364-7
Printed and bound in the United Kingdom

www.dk.com

MIX
Paper | Supporting
responsible forestry
FSC™ C018179

This book was made with Forest
Stewardship Council™ certified
paper – one small step in DK's
commitment to a sustainable future.
Learn more at **www.dk.com/uk/
information/sustainability**

Contents

Introduction

Every school morning started with the same tedious ritual. My mum would quietly approach the side of my bed, gently rub my arm and whisper, 'It's time to get up, love.' I'd roll over, resentful, hoping that I could avoid the world by staying in bed. Then I would lie there for another twenty minutes or so, running through every potential lie my eleven-year-old mind could conjure to get me out of attending. With my inner negotiation over, I would get up.

The only thing that could encourage my unwilling stroll into the living room was the smell of breakfast: cheese on toast with a large cup of silky hot chocolate. Mum knew this was my favourite. She used it as her bargaining tool. She knew that come 8 a.m. we would have to launch into our routine where she pleaded with me to put on my uniform and go to school. I would resist and push back and try all the lies I had generated from my pillow. Eventually I reluctantly agreed: 'Fine! I'll go, Mum. But under one condition. That I don't have to put on my uniform until the very last minute before I cross the school gates.'

The bus journey was spent absorbed in my agonising internal monologue. I tried to convince myself it wasn't that bad. I told myself that every kid must hate school like I did. Although deep down, I knew that if they did, it wasn't for the same reason. The walk up to the gate felt like a walk of shame and, as I got there, I stopped, took off my navy-blue tracksuit top and bottom in exchange for a blue blazer . . . and a skirt. As I walked to class, I watched many of the other girls roll up their waistbands to achieve a shorter look. But I did my best to pull my skirt down, so it fully covered my knees. I thought to myself, *I'm not like the other girls.*

I would walk into my form room, or, as I saw it, four walls solely containing religion and girls, with my head down. Once seated, we would say our Hail Marys and Our Fathers, and I experienced a moment of happiness as my friends said hello to me. That moment was short-lived because the second the school bell rang, all I could think was: *I'm not supposed to be here.*

But this day was different.

That morning, I woke myself up before my mum had the chance to tentatively creep in. I walked into the living room with a beaming smile and, to my mum's surprise, fully dressed in my uniform. On this day, I skipped breakfast and went straight out the door shouting 'Bye!' as it shut behind me. I didn't ask, but I assume she felt a sense of relief knowing that for one day at least, she wouldn't have to face the early morning battle with her eleven-year-old.

It had been years of avoidance. Years of silencing my gut as it screamed of a disconnection. But today, I had had enough. I longed for a sense of belonging, which I knew I could never have with this double life. I had made a decision. If at the end of the day I walked out of my all-girls' school and was still unhappy, I would tell my mum.

I had tried to explain how I felt to her a few times. But I never had the courage to see it through. Now, something in me had shifted. The bell rang at 3.30 p.m., signalling the end of the day, and I knew what I had to do. I walked home with a million thoughts running through my mind. I played out every scenario I could think of, in order to mentally prepare myself for any outcome. My thoughts swirled in the chaos. I thought about how absurd it might sound to her but how deeply innate it felt to me.

Now that I had made this decision, there was no going back. I couldn't spend another day trapped inside this false identity without letting her into my pain. Even with every horrific outcome I imagined, I decided anything would be better than living a lie. More than anything, I wanted happiness. And I knew I couldn't get there if I carried on like this.

I pushed open my front door with shaking hands.

'Mum, I have something to tell you.'

I wonder what my mum had thought before that moment. If she had any theories about why I hated school so much. I wonder if she thought I just wasn't academic and mainstream education wasn't for me. I wonder if she thought we'd picked the wrong school and there was another I'd enjoy more. It was much deeper than that. I couldn't form full sentences or articulate the gravity of my feelings, so rather than explaining it perfectly, I just started talking. Once I started, I didn't stop. Almost eleven years' worth of memories and discomfort poured uncontrollably from my lips into my mum's startled ears.

After a few moments of shock, it became apparent that my speech was being welcomed with kindness. I felt like I could breathe when I realised not only was she listening to me but she was understanding me too. Mum was confused at points. 'So, you're a lesbian?' she asked suspiciously. Before I could deter myself from telling her the truth, I blurted out: 'No, I don't see myself as a girl with a girl, I see myself as a boy, with a girl.'

That was it. The biggest secret of my life was out in the open. I felt raw. I felt vulnerable. But I felt free. It was a life-altering moment, and I knew it. I could tell my mum was doing her best to keep up and process the complex situation. I had had years to sit with my feelings and all she had was a few seconds to respond. After a pause, she said: 'OK, love. I think we should speak to a doctor.'

The next few minutes were spent in a tearful embrace. To feel her hold me when I'd felt so alone in these feelings made my soul smile. She told me that no matter what, she wanted me to be happy. I knew she'd understand me. She was my best friend after all.

She started to realise that my expression as a 'tomboy' was really just the closest I could get to being myself. This was the beginning of a slow acceptance, that she'd always had a boy, but she hadn't known until that day. From this day on, she stopped saying 'OK, love' and started saying 'OK, my boy'.

The journey begins here

The following week, I went with Mum to the GP and she insisted that I repeated everything I had told her. She knew that the only way to proceed healthily was to get it all out into the open. We both hoped that a health professional could help us to get a better understanding of what I was experiencing.

It was the second time I had disclosed my transness and it was greeted with far less warmth and care than the first. The doctor looked at me as if I was speaking to them in a foreign language. It's an understatement to say that they didn't have a clue. After trying to explain my biggest secret to an unreceptive audience, the doctor concluded that I should speak to a therapist. I wanted to ask all the questions I'd been swallowing down over the years, but I didn't. I didn't feel safe, so I stayed silent.

A month on and I was standing outside a mental-health clinic, about to meet my new therapist. The clinician showed me into a small room where she sat down behind a desk and gestured for me to make myself comfortable in an armchair. I started from the beginning once again, this time feeling the familiarity of my story. I spoke for an hour, responding to prompts from the therapist to dig deeper into some feelings. At the end of my appointment, I asked her: 'Why am I here?' She brushed me off, explaining that she was just trying to understand how I was feeling. But I persisted. Eventually she explained that I was expressing similar feelings to those who are diagnosed with gender dysphoria, but it was too early to tell if this was the case for me. I was asked to continue attending therapy for the next twelve weeks and then we would go from there.

After leaving my appointment, I thought about the

classification of transness. This was the first time I realised the category I was being pushed into. It was the first time I asked myself: *Does society view being transgender as a mental disorder?*

Fast forward to May 2019 and the World Health Organisation (WHO) dropped transgender from its list of mental disorders. But the truth is, being trans has never been a mental disorder. We didn't need WHO to tell us that. The labelling made me realise how deeply misunderstood transness was. While a lot has changed since that first appointment, in many ways things are the same.

Transness is more misunderstood than ever before

Over the last ten years, trans rights have been increasingly publicised. But what concerns me is that very few well-informed facts are included in those conversations. A combination of scaremongering in the right-wing press and extreme views on social media have meant people are surrounded by misinformation.

Research by GLAAD,[1] a non-profit organisation focused on LGBTQ advocacy and cultural change, showed that approximately 20 per cent of Americans say they personally know someone who is transgender. In the UK, Stonewall have found that 1 in 4 Britons is close to a trans person.[2] Most people rely on the media for their information. Based on this alone, you could easily think the conversation around being trans is all hormone treatment and bathroom access. If you believed the messages that are presented to you, you'd see: trans women as rapists, trans men motivated by escaping the patriarchy or just as confused, autistic women, and non-binary people as attention seekers. This is simply not true.

If you are a person with a negative view of the trans community, I would love to ask you to consider why that is. Most of us don't deliberately form our opinions, we subconsciously slide into a stance based on the things we're surrounded by. In buying this book you've created an opportunity to be active in your opinion-forming, rather than passive. Here, you may be engaging with perspectives you haven't previously found in mainstream media. Even if you don't change your conclusions, I'm grateful that you took the time to read this book.

Why should it matter to people who aren't trans?

It's easy to brush aside an issue if it doesn't directly affect you. But as you read on, you'll realise these issues are closer to home than you think. At the core of what we are exploring are issues of humanity: access to healthcare and autonomy to make medical-based decisions. What is freedom of speech and what counts as crossing a line into words that will condone harmful behaviour towards others? When we talk about trans people, we are setting the precedent of how we treat people, and challenging the idea that we can pick and choose who 'deserves' access to treatment based on the perceived 'worthiness' of their existence. This book's underlying conversation is one of justice, autonomy, freedom and the ability to self-express. Allyship will always be important and we must remember that all lives are of equal worth. Any person with a good conscience would want us all to be treated equally.

These two facts speak to how greatly needed you are as an ally. Transphobic hate crimes in the UK quadrupled between 2015 and 2020.[3,4] In 2022, Medical News Today reported that: 'Transgender adolescents were 7.6 times as likely to attempt suicide as their cis peers.'[5] The situation is even more concerning for those in the Black trans community who experience homelessness at five times the rate of the general population. An American survey found 20 per cent of Black trans respondents are living with HIV compared to just 2.64 per cent for all transgender responses.[6]

What is cisgender?

I've mentioned the term 'cis' a couple of times already – and on the cover of this book – so it's only right that I offer a definition. You may well already know, but it's always nice to make sure we're starting on the same page, both figuratively and literally. The word 'cisgender' simply means non-trans. It means you identify as the gender you were assigned at birth. There are people who don't like the word because it means that they would no longer be considered the default, or because they misunderstand what it means. It's a word that helps us identify the difference between one another. It's by no means an offensive term and doesn't (and certainly shouldn't) carry negative connotations. Just like someone being tall or short, Black or white, it just is what it is.

That leads me to why I'm writing this book

For many people reading this, it will be the first in-depth insight they will have into the life of a trans person. I want to help you to understand these experiences. I think the more we can humanise the trans experience for those who don't live it, the more empathy we can all share. I'm also a strong believer that we can learn from one another. Maybe my voice will help you find yours in a weird and wonderful way. To that end, this is a vulnerable book for me to write and put out there, so know that my heart is in these pages. I've dug deep to share with you my personal experiences, some of which are steeped in pain.

If you were to use this book as a weapon against other trans people, you've entirely missed the point. My experience may not reflect his/hers/theirs. This is a complex reality for many people and I would never dream of speaking for all of them. I am one man, with one experience, adding my perspective into the arena of trans stories.

Through this book, I'll detail my many hard-learned

lessons. I'll share with you what I went through and what being trans means to me. I'll discuss parts of my transition journey and the process of making decisions around surgery and hormones. I'll also share my perspective on being a Black trans man and how intersectionality affects my experiences. I'll explore what sex looks like in the trans community and the misconceptions that are rife — often thanks to the internet. I'd also love for you to understand the best way you can be an ally and why that's so key, as well as making sure you're up to date with the most inclusive language and that you get why that's so important.

On the topic of language, it is beautiful and facilitates so much, but it has its limits. I've used words that, at the time of publishing, I was comfortable with and are current. But as we all learn and grow, me included, there may be better terms that emerge — just something to keep in mind.

My commitment to you is that I won't shy away from tough topics. I want to give you a book worth reading and I don't believe there's anything to hide. Some of these conversations will exist in a 'grey area' and I'm comfortable with that. In my opinion, it's better to acknowledge than to avoid. I've focused on topics that I believe are of very real concern to cisgender people, and where I can deliver you the most value. I haven't covered every single aspect of a trans person's existence. That said, if there are areas you want to delve into further, there are some other spectacularly insightful books available and I'd encourage you to continue your research.

It's important for me to highlight that I am not a physician, historian or biologist. But I am consulted from time to time by people in these professions so that they can learn from my lived experience. What I am is a trans man who is passionate about advocating for his community and incredibly proud to be a part of it.

It's OK if you feel angry

I don't expect everyone reading this to agree with me. If they did, there would have been no need for the book at all. We have found ourselves in a time where critical thinking and personal research is replaced by half-truths and being swayed by the throng of the crowd. Let's not be people who form our opinions from one tweet, one article, or even one book. But allow each argument to build the bigger picture.

That said, when you come across something that undermines your way of seeing the world, you may feel angry. This is a topic that carries a lot of emotion, and within the passion of our feelings we can shut down and become defensive. My suggestion would be to take a pause and a deep breath. It may help to ask yourself: 'Why is this making me feel angry?' I'm hoping that everyone will approach this with an openness and curiosity. Ready to identify and relinquish biases and come together for the benefit of us all.

Before you turn the page . . .

The key point is, it's not just trans people whose lives are improved by your love and support, it's everyone's. We weren't born to carry around hate, and if we continue down this path it will be our demise.

There will be many types of people who buy this book. Some will already have taken steps to become an ally (thank you) and want to know more. Some may be sceptical about transness and want to learn more before making up their mind (thank you) while others may have been presented with this book by a loved one who is keen for them to truly understand the trans experience (thank you for honouring them by engaging with this).

Being a true ally means questioning, rethinking and unlearning. Trans people face a lot of discrimination both intentionally and unintentionally, so I ask that you open your hearts and minds. I want you to fully immerse yourself not only into the words on these pages but how, if you were a trans person, all of these things would make you feel.

See you on the other side.

1.

Gender
Begins Here

One of the first questions I'm asked when I disclose that I'm trans is: 'How did you know?' The answer, in my personal experience, starts with body dysphoria. Like most things that touch us deeply in good or bad ways, it's hard to describe. Without having lived it yourself, it's difficult for me to convey the feeling in a way that's relatable. But for the sake of your understanding, I'll try. It feels like you are living in somebody else's skin. You're in there, somewhere, but you can't quite find yourself. You have moments of recognition: the odd time when the real you comes out through a genuine smile, a flash of creativity, or a moment of connection that's about the soul and not the body.

Then there are times where it all comes crashing down: hugging my mum but feeling my unwanted boobs touch hers. The slight bounce of my chest as I run. The feeling of back sweat on a bra I did not want to wear. The mental and physical pain of binding my chest to try and flatten it down and create a shape that felt more comfortable. Any reminder that this was the skin I existed in; any reminders of things I did not want.

I'm sure you are aware, but before we move forward there is no harm in clarifying what gender identity actually means. According to Stonewall,[1] it is 'a person's innate sense of their own gender, whether male, female or something else'.

The National Health Service (NHS) in the UK says gender dysphoria is 'a term that describes a sense of unease that a person may have because of a mismatch between their biological sex and their gender identity'.[2] I personally do not like the term 'mismatch' as it implies that the two, sex and gender, have incorrectly come together. For me, 'mix-match' is a better, more accurate description as it's different aspects of that person coming together.

This is common for people in the trans community, and it reflects my experience. It's important to flag that there are trans people who don't feel this way. For some, looking in the mirror doesn't feel like a life-shifting disconnect; they do not feel intense discomfort with the skin they're in. Contrary to what some may believe, gender dysphoria is not a prerequisite to being trans and those that don't experience it are just as valid as those who do.

Under these circumstances, someone might not opt in for physical changes such as surgery, but they might change the way they dress, their name or presentation. Without having lived this myself, I can't explain the situation personally. However, it feels important not to leave you with the impression that everyone who is trans has the same experience.

While we're on that, as an activist I speak to people all the time about transness, and many people confide in me that they recognise the struggle for trans men and women but they just don't understand non-binary people. I get how people land in that place; when your only concept of gender is that it's either/ or, you can understand someone wanting to change from one to the other. But how can you see yourself as both or neither? Some people assume that being non-binary is a stepping stone – a halfway house to being a trans man or woman. This can be true for some but for others their identity feels more fixed or certain. Being non-binary is an identity destination of its own.

My story is one of a trans man and that is different from those who are non-binary. I can only talk about what I personally know. For that reason, I won't be covering the non-binary experience in this book. But there are plenty of non-binary authors and creators to learn from; I'll leave you the names of a few in the recommendations at the end of this book.

For a bit of context: trans and non-binary identities both fall under the trans umbrella. In most cases, trans men are people who were assigned female at birth, raised as a girl but now identify as a man, and trans women are people who were assigned male at birth, were raised as a boy but now identify as being a woman. Non-binary people don't solely identify as being a man or woman; they may see themselves as a combination of the two, as neither, or as something else altogether. The reason they're all categorised as trans is that all three of these groups identify differently from their gender assigned at birth.

If we're talking about my story as a trans man, though, gender dysphoria showed up in force in my early teens, shortly before I began puberty. For years before that, I had feelings of incongruence without mental distress, moments in which my sense of self didn't match the perception of others. I tried not to think about it too much. But this feeling always lingered in the background. Something wasn't *quite* right.

My first memory of this feeling was when I was three years old. Now that I understand biology better, I can see that that makes sense. Experts suggest that children become conscious of the physical differences between boys and girls around the age of two.[3] By four, they have a strong sense of their gender identity and that of those around them. I was a happy and playful child. I always thought that my mum naturally gravitated towards raising me in a genderless way, but in reality I pushed back. She would style me in cute dresses and pigtails with my cheeky smile to finish the look. If you saw my baby pictures, you would have to agree that I was always giving model. Yet, by three years old, I started resisting the girly garms, so she stopped buying them.

As I grew older, there were occasions when I was put in a dress, and I remember feeling the fury run through my veins. I launched into tantrums, feet stomping, shaky hands and tearful pleading; I did not want to wear the clothing that girls wore. I know now what I wouldn't have had the language to express then: to my mind, dress = girl and I wanted as much distance from 'girl' as possible. I wasn't just rejecting the stereotypically feminine outfit, I was rejecting the idea that I was a girl, in the only way I knew how.

In one of our finest stand-offs, Mum put me in *another* dress and I absolutely lost my shit. I was five years old, and we were going to a family wedding. The house was buzzing with people ironing their shirts and styling their hair. Mum knew she would have a battle on her hands with me, so tried to play it smart by making sure I was ready first. She would live to regret that decision.

I pulled up my skirt, sprinted with athlete speed, burst into the bathroom and dived into a fully run bath. The splashes of the water around the ripples of my hem dampened my mum's screams of 'No!' coming from down the hall. I lay back in the warm water, fully clothed, bathing in my genius. Me 1: The Dresses 0.

In my primary-school years, I continued to grow in a conflicting direction. Internally, I felt increasingly settled with my Kenny identity. But to everyone else, I was Kelsey: a girl who was increasingly 'tomboyish'. People got used to me without asking questions. They expected me to show up in tracksuits and trainers rather than skirts and dresses. I copied the other boys and looked to them for my example. I used the boys' toilets and changing rooms, which raised the eyebrows of some teachers.

I once asked my mum why I was called Kelsey when it was so girly. In fairness, she put up a good fight for Kelsey being gender-neutral. She pointed out Kelsey Grammer (from *Frasier*) and Kelsey Stevenson (a Canadian tennis player) who were men and shared my name. It was a nice try on her behalf, but I was absolutely not buying it. Although I love the name Kelsey, much like my supposed gender, I didn't feel like it accurately reflected who I was.

Slowly, over time, the ball began to drop. The friction between my internal world and the outer world became louder the older I got. I became self-conscious because I didn't lean into the 'girly' hobbies of my peers. People thought the 'tomboy phase' would slip away and I would move on to another stage, but I didn't. Being trans is not a phase. As a young child, my world was naturally small. I spent time with family and school friends. I was in a safety bubble of people who knew me well. Growing up meant I was forced to burst that bubble. Increased independence led to new environments and new people. I was suddenly faced with people from after-school clubs, my local football team and in church, and it became apparent that I wasn't meeting their expectations of a little girl.

The other children took me as I was. I had to go toe to toe with the occasional 'Why do you dress like a boy?' But on the whole, it was adults who made it clear they thought I was doing something wrong. They would ask why I didn't like to wear dresses and would look incredulous when I told them it was because 'Boys don't wear dresses'. The discrepancy between my world and theirs was becoming too much for me. I knew I was a boy, but I also knew others weren't seeing me that way. I didn't understand why they wouldn't just listen to me. When it all got too much, I would curl up on the floor of my mum's makeshift walk-in wardrobe and cry.

As a child, I didn't know what transness was, but even without the language to put to it, I knew it felt true. I wasn't delusional, I understood the difference between boys and girls. I just felt like somehow society got it wrong when categorising me. When I got to ten years old, I discovered the online world and it brought me a sense of comfort. I could be anyone I wanted to be there. I could create avatars with a body the way I liked, and a new name to match. I became obsessed with an online virtual world called 'Habbo Hotel', playing for hours every day after school in my digital sanctuary. For a month I called their premium phone line every day to collect Habbo credits (the game's currency). When the £300 bill arrived, you better believe my mum kicked my little butt. I fucked up big time with that one.

My days in primary school were coming to an end and I was anxious about my next step. The summer before starting at secondary school, I felt the tension build up. I was less worried about whether the kids would like me or if I'd get good grades. I was just worried that they would think I was weird. I was desperate to go to our local school. A load of my friends were already signed up and the uniform was a simple black tracksuit with a red and white logo. My mum was convinced that I could go somewhere with higher academic achievement. She picked out a Catholic all-girls' school that reported excellent grades every year. We argued about it a lot. But, desperate to give me the best possible start, she wouldn't budge. At the open day they presented me with my uniform, a blue blazer and a skirt. I wanted to cry.

Shortly after this was when I came out to my mum and a slew of doctor's appointments, misdiagnoses, painful conversations and those twelve weeks of therapy followed. The process of finally getting the right diagnosis took eight brutal years. After that, and only after that, was I prescribed testosterone. There's a misconception in the media that the NHS is handing out meds to pre-teens all willy-nilly, but that's not the case. Even being prescribed puberty blockers, which happened the year before my diagnosis, was only granted to me because I had become suicidal.

Don't get me wrong, I'm pleased that there are thorough checks in place. But I believe there is a safer way to assess someone's eligibility than the one I went through. I had to meet with countless medical professionals. It was emotionally torturous having to relive traumatic events in order to prove myself eligible for gender-affirming treatment. I was made to spew out my deepest pain over and over again; repeatedly explaining my feelings of disconnect between my body and sense of self and constantly rehashing how long I had felt this way and since when. Then I had to wait to find out if I'd been 'convincing enough' and was indeed viewed in the eyes of a cis person as trans. I felt completely out of control waiting for a diagnosis from someone who had no idea what it felt like. Can you imagine spending seven years explaining to multiple health professionals who you are, only to have them fire more questions at you and do nothing to help? Time that I could have spent being happier was stolen from me. I wish that those appointments had more forward momentum, where my dignity was prioritised. Instead, I felt I was subjected to a series of interrogations.

Being diagnosed gave me a sense of peace. I had the concrete answer I was looking for. I was finally heard. But it also made me question my entire existence. How is being trans even possible? I needed to understand more about it to feel settled in my identity.

A brief overview of Western sex and gender

I knew what being transgender meant on paper, but I needed to understand the reasons why or how it can happen. For a long time, I assumed that if your gender and the sex that you were assigned at birth weren't the same, there was something wrong with you. I thought it meant we were in a group of unwell people with this uncommon mental-health disorder. Which makes sense given how we are taught about transness: it's always from a very medical lens. To better understand this mix-match, I hit the books.

Wading through some heavy texts and scientific research was a task and a half, but the more I understood about biology, transness and its historical context, the more I learned that it's actually a natural occurrence. Let me take you on the journey . . .

In recent years, the World Health Organization (WHO) has helped to develop mainstream understanding of transness[4]. They started with the semantics. The words they used mattered and they recognised that. They've ditched outdated terms like 'transsexualism' and 'gender identity disorder' to a phrase that feels much closer to the truth 'gender incongruence'. They said: 'This reflects current knowledge that trans-related and gender diverse identities are not conditions of mental ill-health, and that classifying them as such can cause enormous stigma.' Ain't that the truth!

I'm pleased that the stigma is being recognised, and I hope reframing our understanding will help us step away from a world that continues to medicalise sex and gender. We do also need a diagnosis, as without it we wouldn't have access to necessary medical interventions.

Even the phrasing I used when I first came out, 'I was born in the wrong body,' made it sound like I thought there was something wrong with me. That's partly because it was the only language I had at the time and partly because I did think it made me unwell given what medical category 'transgender' used to live in.

As I've already mentioned, being transgender was previously associated with mental illness. The world has plenty of people who still believe this to be the case. Throughout history, LGBTQ+ identities have been labelled 'mentally ill'. It was only in 1974 that the American Psychiatric Association stopped classifying *homosexuality* as a mental disorder. Internationally recognised health expert and author of *The Vagina Book*, Dr Jenn Conti, said: 'We've historically misclassified a lot of conditions in medicine because of a combination of stigma, fear and misunderstanding.'[5]

The starting point for building an understanding of transness is to see the difference between gender and sex. These terms have historically been used interchangeably but they aren't the same. Speaking about them as if they are reinforces the idea that the only natural state is when they are in a certain alignment.

So, let's talk about sex, baby! (I know, I'm sorry, but I couldn't help it.) In humans, 'sex' is defined by various biological characteristics that scientists and doctors use to categorise us as female and male. When it comes to gender, that's the innate sense of who a person is. This could be man, woman, other or neither. When it comes to gender, that's a social construction! Every society has its own ideas of what classifies as masculine or feminine, and it uses those ideas to put gendered rules and expectations on everyone. But everyone also has an innate sense of who they are. That could be man, woman, other or neither.

Sex and gender have classically been conflated. The second a baby pops out, the midwife looks at their visible genitalia (just one example of a person's sex characteristics) and announces: 'It's a boy!' (gender). Many people think that the idea that sex and gender are different is a recent one. But it was actually back in 1955 that the distinction was made, and even then, scientists still thought your sex and gender were *supposed* to align, and if they didn't then something was wrong with you. A lot of people still believe that a person's biological sex, which is only one factor, solely determines their gender. And in my experience, if the two don't align, you can be told you're confused, unwell or that your very existence isn't real.

The sex-equals-gender calculation has been flawed from the get-go. There are plenty of people who are born with biological variations in their sex development that could see them fall into either the male or female category. But they are assigned a gender, and they are raised as either a boy or girl. Western culture oversimplifies sex and gender.

The making of babies is wild – and I'm not talking about what happens in the bedroom. Did you know the odds of you being born is one in 400 trillion? A myriad of different elements and developmental stages all piece together to make you the complex, passionate and exciting person you are. Then you're born and boxed into one of two categories: male or female. One of the main arguments against trans identities is that 'binary sex is a biological reality which you can't change, and that's all that matters'. But is sex that simple, and is it actually binary? Let's break down how complex sex actually is.

I'll be real, I'm no biologist so I've borrowed the help of my talented friend Anick, who is a writer and researcher with a degree in law, and further studies in children's rights, advanced social work and psychology. Here's what they had to say: 'Chromosomal sex refers to the sex chromosomes we inherit. These cannot be changed. They come in distinct patterns which could be XX, XY, XO, XXY, XY/XX.' So not just the XX or XY that most of us are familiar with (although these are the most common).

I know this is heavy stuff but bear with me. Anick continues: 'There are also factors like the sex-determining region Y gene (SRY) gene which is important in determining how the body will respond.' This is basically a gene on the Y chromosome that is responsible for kicking off the male sex determination, but can also in rare situations appear in a person who has XX.

Anick went on to explain the different types of sex we determine. They said:

Gonadal sex is determined by our internal genitalia, the ovaries and/or testes, which produce different sex hormones. Everybody responds in a unique way. While we have oversimplified gonadal sex by labelling some hormones as 'male' and others as 'female', in reality we all have varying levels of the same hormones which react in our bodies in different ways. Then, anatomical sex is often determined by our external genitalia, whether someone has a penis or a vulva. These can come in many different shapes and sizes, irrespective of chromosomal or gonadal sex. This is the way the vast majority of people's sex is assigned at birth.

For most people, anatomical, gonadal and chromosomal correspond to each other, as well as to their gendered identity. For most people, all of these three align, along with gender identity, but this isn't the case for everyone.

This shines a light on the three different aspects of us that build into our gender identity. When we're born, the doctor will designate us as female or male based on what they can observe: anatomical sex. But as we now know, there is so much more going on internally. These three elements aren't always aligned and, although it's uncommon, for some people gonadal, anatomical and chromosomal sex don't all line up. This is scientifically referred to as difference of sex development (DSD) and is often pathologized – meaning it's made medical.

Being born with intersex traits is a core example of the fluidity that sex has to offer. The term 'intersex' is used to describe those who are born with an uncommon variation in their sexual characteristics. There are forty different variations known in medicine at present. It's difficult to know the number of people born with intersex traits as people debate the meaning and globally we don't record intersex data.

People discover that they are intersex in several ways. Some have so-called ambiguous genitalia at birth. But others may find out later in life when they begin puberty and their body develops in apparently atypical ways. And some people never find out at all.

There are other, beautiful variations on the binary norms that we're conditioned to believe are incorrect. There are women with Mayer-Rokitansky-Küster-Hauser (MRKH), who are born without a vagina or uterus (or the underdevelopment of them). While men with Persistent Müllerian Duct Syndrome (PMDS) have cis-expected external genitalia but also have a uterus and fallopian tubes. You may have never heard of an even more rare variation called Ovotesticular, where an individual is born with a combination of ovarian/testicular tissue.

Yet when mainstream conversations strike up about sex, only two options are acknowledged and the fluidity that exists is brushed under the rug. So much so that when someone is born who doesn't fit neatly into the 'female' or 'male' box, the first reaction is to try and 'correct' this by enforcing the binary gender and expected, or more desirable, sex characteristics.

Let's look at what happens when a baby is born with visibly intersex anatomy. Some are operated on in order to place them in one of the binary sex categories and their parents then raise them according to the new, binary sex they've been assigned. In a study in Lübeck conducted between 2005 and 2007 by a German research group, 81 per cent of 439 individuals had been subjected to surgeries due to their intersex diagnosis.[6] Let's remember while we review those figures that there are not always adverse health implications or additional risks for being born intersex. Unnecessarily operating on these individuals can create risk.[7] Some variations do require treatment at birth – for example, if a child can't go to the toilet easily – but often, surgery isn't medically necessary.

The initial intention of stabilising these children is to prevent them from having future mental- and physical-health problems.

But it doesn't work. Almost half of the same study group said they had psychological problems and two-thirds said they had sexual problems in adulthood that they associated with their history of surgical treatment.

Unlike intersex people, trans people these days often find ourselves desperately seeking treatment rather than trying to avoid it. We can be offered hormone replacement therapy (HRT), or as we now call them, gender-affirming hormones. These are a positive treatment option for any trans person experiencing gender dysphoria who wants to alleviate some of that discomfort. But it isn't always used as a helpful tool. In some countries, a trans person is only allowed to live as their true gender if they are diagnosed as having a 'gender-identity disorder', take HRT and are sterilised by having all surgeries. It's mandatory. In other words, you can switch from one binary gender to another as long as you take medication to help you neatly slot into your new category. Talk about keeping up the gender norms.

Not every trans person feels they must take hormones or have surgery. It's important that people get to make their own decisions and follow a path that is tailored to their needs.

It's a big jump for a cis person to unlearn what they thought they knew about sex and gender and acknowledge that sex is complicated and doesn't always determine gender.

Although for the majority of the population, the three aspects of sex all line up, and match our gender identity, it's not the case for all.

More than that, we need to move away from seeing the 'realness' of someone's gender through the lens of biological sex. A man's gender is just as real even if he wasn't assigned male at birth, and doesn't have (or hasn't always had) the sex characteristics we label as male. The same goes for women, and for the whole spectrum of non-binary identities.

Gender is a visceral feeling, a matter of the inner being that is unaligned with biological sex. How we move forward in society requires a more holistic approach to rules in competitive sport, healthcare, law and much more. But don't freak out about those things, it's all doable. We've built this system, we can remodel it to be inclusive for everyone.

When we strip away the assumptions, labels and interpretations from all our complicated sexual characteristics, we're left with just this: there are two reproductive systems that fuse in order to make a baby, eggs and sperm. That's it – and we have the freedom to interpret and label those bodies however we want. There is nothing to fear in freedom. Our existence provides cis people with the opportunity to expand their view of gender and its expression. A person who is secure in themselves would never feel threatened by this growth in their understanding of sex and gender, they would welcome it.

Sex, gender and trans identities across time and space

There is this myth that being trans and/or non-binary is a new concept, but historians would beg to differ. I want to look at some examples of gender diversity that have existed for hundreds and, in some cases, thousands of years. Though the history is complex, in some times and places a duality of gender has been celebrated and even seen as godlike. This is especially true in cultures which think about gender differently from the Western world – we can learn a lot from them.

For starters, let me transport you over to Thailand. You might have heard of the *kathoeys* or 'ladyboys'. These days, the Thai word is translated as 'transgender women' but that's not the full story. Back in the day, the term was used to describe intersex people, but it has since evolved. Though *kathoeys* can face social discrimination, especially in the workplace, there's also a deep cultural respect for this group. Many Thai people view *kathoeys* as being a sex of their own and there are *kathoeys* who would agree.

Indigenous North Americans have people that they would refer to as 'two-spirit' – I love this term. These individuals are often highly regarded in their communities. In many of these cultures, they are believed to have the spirit of both man and woman, and because of that they are seen as more gifted than others. They are often offered the most important roles in society, with jobs as healers, matchmakers and counsellors. Some interpret their own sex and gender by allowing their spirit to speak for them.

In Native Hawaiian and Tahitian culture they recognise three genders: *wahine* (women), *kane* (men) and mãhu, who are seen as in the middle, many of whom were assigned male at birth (AMAB). Much like two-spirit people, they are seen to embrace both femininity and masculinity. They are highly respected and hold important roles in their communities like teachers, priests and healers. They are seen as keepers of traditional culture and lineages. Parents go to them and ask them to name their children.

Back east in India, you have *hijras*, a group that includes both intersex and trans people together, and who often dress in a 'feminine' way. They are seen as a third gender and are legally recognised in their country. They play an important role in Hindu texts and are thought of as people who can bring blessings to others, like fertility and prosperity. Then there are the *baklâs* in the Philippines, *femminielli* in traditional Neapolitan culture and many more.

Devastatingly, a lot of these countries lost their ability to live life this way when they were colonised. On the surface, gender can feel like a simple method of self-expression. But it's more than that. It wields more power. Historically, it's been used to govern people. For example, the Dawes Act of 1887.

This law allowed the President of the United States to divide up the land inhabited by Indigenous Native American communities and assign ownership of each part to a family within that community. When you don't spend too long analysing it, this can sound great. They would have legal ownership rights over their land. But, far from protecting the Indigenous peoples, it completely ripped them from their way of life. These communities had a communal lifestyle that was based on stewardship. The Dawes Act introduced private property. This split their ownership from people into individuals and threw them into the world of capitalism.

With this dramatic shift in lifestyle came the reinforcement of Western gender roles. The government assigned property rights to the person they deemed to be head of the household, and in true Western fashion this was: the man. Suddenly Indigenous people, free from any binary gender norms, had to decide whether they were a man or a woman in order to be granted access to their own land. And so the white colonial leaders achieved their goal: introducing 'society' to 'the savages' by forcing them to turn away from their own beautiful heritage to be absorbed by the dominant culture of the time.

Why do trans people exist?

Whether we like it or not, the queer community has been alive and well and around for all of time. It's not just humans who embrace the non-binary and fluidity. There are gender-swapping fish,[8] genderqueer lions,[9] birthing male seahorses,[10] partially asexual ants[11] and many others. Asking why transness exists is like asking why cisness exists. Just because one is less common doesn't invalidate it.

If that's not enough to convince you that trans people are a natural occurrence, then I'm happy to delve further into the research with you. In looking into this, I found a TED Talk by

American doctor James O'Keefe that summed things up perfectly for me. In the presentation titled 'Homosexuality: It's about survival – not sex',[12] Dr O'Keefe opens up about his son Jimmy coming out as gay with a touching story. Then he explains that he was worried for his son's safety and family prospects. He then hits with a blow by saying that homosexuality seems to be a real self-defeating non-productive strategy, given that statistically gay men have 80 per cent fewer children than straight men. Hold tight, though, because his reasoning is about to turn a corner.

Next, Dr O'Keefe explains that, throughout history, in every culture and animal species, homosexuality has been a small but distinct subgroup. Now we're getting to the good stuff. He continues: 'If this [homosexuality] were a genetic error, natural selection should have long ago culled this from the gene pool.' He continues: 'E. O. Wilson, probably the greatest evolutionary biologist since Darwin himself, says: "Homosexuality gives advantages to the group by specialised talents and unusual qualities of personality. So, a society that condemns homosexuality harms itself."' It's towards the end of the talk that he explains that the same principle can be applied to trans people.

In this speech, I heard expertise and research confirm everything I knew to be true in my heart. The queer community, including the trans community, is special. My favourite phrase of the talk is: 'Diversity is nature's secret weapon.' It truly is. Life has always needed diversity, it's a key part of our survival as humans. Trans people are a natural necessity of human variation.

Trans people have such a unique insight into all things human. Some of us had a double gender experience which can give us a deeper level of empathy for others. For example, I relate to some of the discrimination women face because at times we share a similar struggle. Sometimes we share the same fight, like when the landmark abortion case *Roe v. Wade* was overturned in the US. But at the same time, I can relate to men's issues, like not feeling you can talk to anyone about your inner, emotional world, or feeling the pressure of showing up well in my masculinity.

We may be a small part of the population, but we are mighty. We are mighty in how we positively impact those around us. We are mighty in the way we stand together as a collective family. We are mighty and strong because we stripped ourselves of everything we knew in order to become a more true version of ourselves.

2.

Black
and Trans

In writing a book that draws so heavily on my personal experiences, there was one topic I felt a real responsibility to speak well on. Being Black. No one put that pressure on me, other than myself. I just know that opportunities for Black trans activists to write books published by one of the largest publishing houses in the world don't come around often. And I don't want to waste mine.

My activism over the years has been focused on my identity as a member of the trans community. Don't get me wrong, though. I'd always talk about my heritage when the opportunity presented itself. But let's be real, that isn't very often. In many ways that makes sense. I've endured far more discrimination on account of my transness than I have for being mixed race. But it always felt quite odd.

There have been times, when working with brands that shall remain nameless, when I've been deliberately instructed not to reference race. They'd make soft remarks like: 'I think it best if we focus on one subject and really drive that point home.' Truth is, some people, especially those who are new to social justice, struggle to comprehend it – the concept of someone being discriminated against for more than one part of their identity. How those discriminations may overlap to negatively affect someone's life is complex, and is difficult to recognise with new eyes.

This book was in its early stages when the Black Lives Matter movement kicked off with renewed energy in the States and subsequently the UK and globally. The unforgivable murder of George Floyd had just happened. Breonna Taylor, a Black woman, shared the same fate two months prior, and both were at the hands of the police, the people who are meant to protect us. Like many other Black people, I felt enraged. I spent the following three months intensively watching the protests unfold over social media. I was glued to my screen. Gradually, after weeks of what felt like inhaling trauma, I started to emotionally disconnect.

Ingesting that amount of tragedy, grid post after grid post, article after article, left me feeling numb. My heart was not equipped to experience that much heartbreak. Their pain became my pain. I'd think to myself, any one of these articles speaking on the mistreatment, abuse and murder of Black people could have been about me or someone I love. All because of the colour of their skin.

This time brought up uncomfortable feelings for me. At times I'd feel guilty. I recognised that I was safer than other Black people. I knew I held privilege within my Blackness because I'm mixed race and have lighter skin. This raised feelings of guilt around my transness too as I am passing – people wouldn't look at me and assume that I am trans, which makes for an easier life with less discrimination. I was aware that, compared to some, I had it easy.

I had to ask myself: should I be doing more anti-racism work? I know now that I can't fight every battle, and I won't, but it took some soul-searching for me to feel comfortable with that reality.

Growing up

I'm half English and half Jamaican, but I've always identified more with my Black side than my white. My desire to be seen in my Blackness is something that historically wasn't a choice for us. In the days of enslavement, there was a rule that ensured mixed-race people stayed on the Black side of the Black–white divide.[1] One drop of Black blood meant that person was given the same legal and social treatment as a Black person, regardless of how mixed or light-skinned they were. So, although I am equal parts Black and white, being mixed would've meant Black and today that legacy still holds.

Despite this oppressive history, I love being Black. Regardless of the many obstacles we've had to overcome, we've always come out on top and shining. Our level of strength and resilience speaks for itself. I love our music, our food, our language and linguistic quirks. I love the silky tone of my skin when I get a tan. And most importantly I love the combination of being Black and trans. It makes me feel unique and that I can offer endless value to the world because of it. I'm a proud Black trans man.

My dad is my Black parent and my relationship with him was really tough. I didn't know much about him. Even before I came out as trans, our connection felt distant. I tried not to take it personally. His withdrawn parenting style didn't come as a surprise to me. I have ten siblings on his side of my family. Two boys, seven girls and me. I'm the second youngest and I originally thought that he was just tired of raising children by the time he reached me. But when I asked my siblings how present he was in their lives, they all reported similar experiences. This isn't usual. I know many friends who have a Black dad who wasn't very present. He was a part of that generation of Black dads, specifically Caribbean, who left the parenting to the mothers.

I wouldn't say he raised me, but even so, he was there throughout my life. Physically, he showed up to events and spent time around me, but he didn't invest nearly as much energy into me as my mum did. He wasn't consistent and would show up some days and skip others. Often when he did show up, he'd take me to do all the cool shit like going to the local funfairs, but when it was time to do the hard parenting you couldn't see him for dust. It was my mum who taught me the difference between right and wrong, instilled good values, guided me through life's challenges and encouraged me to follow my wildest dreams. Bless my mum, she did all that. What a superwoman.

My dad didn't speak about his past much. He always came

across as a man with more focus on the present. As I get older, I find myself acting the same way. I think that's the healthy way to cope for people who have endured as many emotional wounds as I have. Maybe his reasons were the same.

Most people knew him by his nickname, 'House', but I called him Papa. He had a swagger about him. He was extremely charming and the ladies loved him – well, he did have ten kids so you probably worked that one out. He was always in corduroy trousers and Clarks, often topping off his look with a Rasta cap filled by his long dreads. He smelled like the perfect blend of Old Spice and weed, and I always found it comforting; my younger sister, Maresha, describes it as earthy. He constantly made this clicking noise with this tongue and the top of his mouth as he cleared his sinuses. It was a comforting sound that meant I'd always hear him coming before he stepped into the room.

As distant as he may have been, he would often pop by and ensure his presence was known. Most of the time it was just his attempt at a booty call with my mum. I'd hear him flirting and her giggling. In those moments I was happy that they were happy. On every visit, he'd knock on my bedroom door, take a seat at the end of my bed and ask me how I was. This became our ritual. I loved those bite-size moments with him. As a young child, I was excited to tell my parents about what I'd been up to, and in return he always managed to make being an adult sound so boring. It didn't matter, it was a back-and-forth exchange that I learned to love because it was with him.

Let's face it, no parent is perfect. I can't change the past and I always try to hold onto the positive memories. But I would be lying if I said I hadn't wondered how my life would have been if he had taken a more active role and invested in me emotionally. However, regardless of everything, he was a loving parent. I appreciated that about him.

There were big moments of friction in Papa's and my relationship. Moments when I thought because I was trans I'd no longer have a dad. Our journey was a really bumpy one. I always hoped we would find common ground in the end.

For a short period when I was fifteen, I had moved in with Papa. My mum and I were arguing intensely because I had become a real troublesome teen. I was struggling to process all the emotions that came up with puberty and not wanting my body to change in the way it was. I hated most parts of myself. I was smoking weed, picking fights, hanging with gangs, partying; coming home when I wanted and generally treating everyone around me like shit. You name it, I did it. It's not because that was who I was, or who I wanted to be. I was just unhappy, and as a teen I didn't know what to do with those emotions. The only thing that got me through was my belief that I was indeed a good person and that, with time, things would get better.

Moving in with Dad was a last resort. I felt comfortable around him in a way that you do with someone when you share 50 per cent of their DNA. There was a bond between us but we hadn't explored it. And that moment wasn't the right time to delve into our connection, as I was taking steps towards my transition.

I knew that by living with him it would all come out. He had a one-bedroom flat located in Kilburn. It was fairly small but the perfect size for him. He let me take the bedroom and set himself up in the living room. His flat was consistently clean, which I liked, and he pretty much only cooked and ate Caribbean food, which I double liked. I didn't end up staying for long, but it was long enough for Papa to see how my appearance, mannerisms and behaviours had become far more masculine.

Two years before this, I had come out to my other loved ones. They welcomed my new name and pronouns with open arms.

To them, it didn't come completely out of the blue. Most of my family were aware that I wanted to transition, and my friends already saw me as a boy, so they just had to update the semantics. But something stopped me from having that conversation with Papa. I knew I had to tread carefully with him.

I opted for a 'soft launch'. I made remarks like 'I just feel more like a boy than a girl' instead of 'I am a boy, not a girl.' He could see things were happening and knew that people had started to call me by my new name, Kenny. My mum felt good about these changes. She was seeing me become increasingly more comfortable and confident in my skin. It was a sign to her that I was on the right track. I hoped that Papa would notice the positive changes in my mood and mental health and would react in the same way. But that's not the response I got.

Mum would often act as a buffer between us. She would fill him in on how I was feeling and the changes I was going through. She was the one who first told him about the dysphoria I was experiencing. I'm grateful that she was his first touch point with it all. It meant that she soaked up his initial negative reaction without exposing me to it. Sometimes she would go into the other room to brief him over the phone. Or if he came to the house, she would walk him away from the front door to prepare him before he walked in and saw me. There was one occasion when they thought they'd gone far enough away that I wouldn't overhear them, but I did.

I heard her pleading with him to be more understanding. She said: 'This is our child, and we have to love him regardless.' To which he just replied: 'Her. We have to love *her* regardless.' He didn't understand and I think he didn't want a queer child. It scared him. The unknown can be scary. Like many parents, I think he believed I was going through a phase.

When I look at Papa's upbringing and context, it becomes less surprising that he responded as he did. He was born and raised in Kingston, Jamaica. When he was growing up, Jamaica was a fiercely homophobic place. As far as the majority were concerned, it was wrong to be a lesbian, a gay man, bisexual or transgender. This was reinforced by anti-queer legislation.

In 1864, Jamaica introduced The Offences Against the Person Act, which is also known as the 'buggery' law. According to the American group Human Rights First: 'Homosexual acts are illegal in Jamaica, levying sentences of up to ten years of imprisonment with hard labour for those convicted.'[2] The phrasing of the legislation is sufficiently open that it doesn't technically discriminate against one group. It criminalises the act of anal sex, not of being homosexual. If you're hoping times have changed in sunny Jamaica, you may find yourself disappointed. At the time of publication, this law was still in place. Additionally, in 2006 *Time* magazine suggested Jamaica was 'the most homophobic place on earth'[3] and in 2016 the BBC claimed the country was one of the most transphobic in the world.[4]

The Caribbean as a whole continues to be a hostile environment for the queer community, another legacy of colonialism. Eleven of the thirteen independent countries in the region have laws against male–male sexual activity, while female–female sexual activity is illegal in seven.[5]

This was the backdrop in front of which my dad developed his attitudes. But he also had a personal connection with the issue. Papa's brother lived in Jamaica and tragically died by suicide after years of trying to be accepted as a gay man. My heart breaks when I think about the low place he must have been in to make that decision. It should never have come to that.

Papa felt the weight of his brother's death heavily. I know it troubled his conscience. As much as he didn't want to have a queer child and struggled to accept me, he knew the grave consequences of making someone feel isolated and unwelcome.

He never wanted history to repeat itself. He loved me and wanted the best for me, but even so, our relationship became strained.

During that brief period while we lived together, we kept our conversations light. He would ask me about my day and what I wanted for dinner. He didn't ask me questions about my gender or sexuality. The shit hit the fan when I had been there for a few weeks. I got tired of the surface-level talk and wanted to pull his head out of the sand. He could see me changing in front of his very eyes and I felt like he needed to come to terms with it. He didn't call me Kenny or 'he' but wasn't quick to call me Kelsey or 'she' either. In most cases he would just avoid referring to me altogether.

I felt increasingly angry about it but I had grown in confidence and understanding of myself and was ready to fully share this with him. I didn't feel afraid any more. I sat him down and, though I wanted to stay calm, I really wasn't. I told him the full extent of my feelings. I made sure he knew that this was no phase. I explained that I was completely committed to transitioning, and that I had an unwavering need for testosterone and surgery.

It blew up. Partly because I came in hot and heavy, partly because it was always going to. What I remember most from that argument wasn't what he said, but what he didn't. There were no words of reassurance, no 'I love you's. He just met me with a blank stare. I suppose he was in shock. I had hardly ever raised my voice to the man, yet here I was, standing strong, roaring at him that this was me and there was nothing he could do about it.

It was at that moment that he realised what I was saying was true. I knew my words had made an impact on him – I could see it. Even so, he dismissed me and that only served to make me more angry. I had to walk away. But I did it swearing and slamming doors.

We didn't speak for the next few days, until an evening when I came home to find that he'd fallen asleep early on the sofa. Still fuming at my treatment, I took the keys to his beloved BMW 3 series, also known as his pride and joy. I wanted to hurt him. So, I drove it around trying to pick up a girl I had a crush on. I was just nearing her house when I picked up my phone to check her address and saw twelve missed calls from my papa and a slew of furious texts. He was mad as fuck. He sent me back to my mum's the next day.

Papa and I never spoke about that incident again. I think he wanted to avoid the hard parenting that fell to my mum. When I got back to hers, she sat me down and asked why I had done it. I didn't say much, but she knew I was playing up because I wasn't happy in my relationship with my dad. But in true Mum fashion, she did laugh at how ridiculous the whole situation had been. I said I wouldn't do it again and we left it there.

I turned sixteen in the summer of 2010 and with that milestone age I felt ready to take the next steps in my social transition. I had asked my mum if I could cut my hair short when I was fourteen, but she asked me to give it another couple of years before we pulled the trigger on such a visible change. She was protective of me and there were already moments when I was bullied for dressing in a masculine way. She didn't want this next step to open me up to more bad treatment. I assured her that I had tiny muscles to fight off the bullies now (that made her giggle). I also told her that if the world was unkind to me, I would always have her love to come home to. I was ready.

Cutting my hair to a new slick skin fade wasn't about the hair itself. It was my way of drawing a line between my former life as Kelsey and my new life as Kenny.

Despite having the conversation with Mum, I didn't talk it through with Papa before performing the big cut. A couple of days later, he dropped by on one of his regular visits. Before fully opening the door to invite him in, my mum lowered her voice and tried to explain that I had made changes since the last time we saw each other. I could hear her nervousness as she tried to prepare him.

I knew the conversation I was about to have was going to be a difficult one and I had built myself up for it. I knew that this conversation had the potential to end our relationship for good. That wasn't what I wanted, but I knew it was an option.

Papa wanted to go to the shop before coming into the house, but I couldn't wait so I ran to join him in his car. I pulled my hood over my newly shaven head before throwing myself onto the back seat of his BMW. I said, 'Papa, I have something to tell you.' He stayed silent, not inviting me to continue but not telling me to leave. He waited. I had sat him down before to give him updates about my transition that I thought he'd find upsetting. My heart would punch the inside of my ribcage and I'd have to push through the nervousness in order to deliver my news. This time was different though. My palms weren't clammy and my mind was clear. I wasn't filled with anxiety. I was filled with a deep, plummeting dread. I felt at peace with my decision to shave my head and my decision to tell him. I knew both were right. But much like phoning a partner to tell them you want to end things, I felt the weight of a hard conversation sitting in my stomach, pulling me down into the leather upholstered chairs.

I just said it: 'I've cut my hair and changed my name.' He giggled. He fucking giggled. I looked him dead in the eye and said: 'I'm serious, Dad.' He knew I was serious because I never called him Dad. I took a deep breath and pulled the hood off my head to reveal my skin fade.

Papa could speak Jamaican patois fluently but he rarely used it. I heard the occasional phrase when he was around other Caribbeans and sometimes a word here or there. When he saw my shaved head, he broke into full patois without pausing for breath. That could only mean one thing: Papa was mad as fuck. His tone went so deep that I could only understand half of the words he was saying. His vexed facial expression filled in the gaps.

This was the biggest disagreement we ever had. My mum reassured me: 'He'll come around.' I believed her. I had to. The other option was heartbreaking. It took us a while to speak again, but I was OK with that. I understood that he needed time to get his head around it all. For years I had known that I wanted to transition, and maybe he would need the same amount of time to adjust.

The following few years were punctuated with major milestones and major setbacks in our relationship. It started to feel like a dance: two steps forward, one step back. In my eyes this was a success; it was much better than the complete ignorance he had shown before. He started to make an effort. On one occasion, I swung by his house to say hello and he had a new friend over. I didn't stick around but as I walked past the door of the living room where she was sitting, I gave her a polite smile and said 'Bye'. Papa stopped me before I could leave and asked if he could introduce me properly before I left. I agreed and we walked back into the lounge together, where he told her: 'This is my second youngest, K.'

That may not sound like much to you, but when he called me K it meant the world. He had let go of Kelsey. He was trying and we were taking baby steps. My heart felt full. I cried happy tears that day. I knew we were a long way away from his accepting me as his son and using he/him pronouns, but this gesture was special. I made sure to thank him and let him know how much it meant to me.

The final hurdle of our relationship came when I was

twenty. It was the day I had top (chest) surgery. I decided not to tell Papa I was going on the operating table, just as I hadn't told him I was going to town with the clippers. When I thought about it, my brain instantly reminded me of his reaction four years earlier and I couldn't do it.

My mum wanted to come with me but I insisted I went alone. She had been my biggest support, defender, champion and ally. She'd been by my side for every appointment, but there came a point when I had to stand on my own two feet. This was when her little boy became a man. It was my time.

We settled on my cousin Carla coming with me to the hospital. It was a good thing we did; I wasn't making it home to London all the way from Brighton by myself. When I came round after surgery I asked her to take a photo of me to commemorate the moment. I was so high on painkillers that instead of grabbing my snapback, I grabbed the hospital's cardboard sick bowl and threw it on my head instead! Thankfully I made it home safely, and got the shot with the correct hat.

Once I was home and she knew the operation had gone well, Mum called Papa to let him know that I had undergone the surgery. He dropped everything and rushed over. As he arrived, I was standing on the road outside my house, topless and strapped up with blood-stained bandages. I was finally letting my bare chest feel the wind. It was a moment of pure gender euphoria. As he approached, he said: 'You look happy.' I replied: 'I've never been happier, Papa.'

Everything changed after that. I'm sure he had come over to disapprove of my decision, but when he saw me standing there, on cloud nine, he changed his mind. I'm sure that he silently still struggled with his preconditioned beliefs about transness, but since that moment, I was fully accepted as his third son.

I don't believe my story is a unique one. I think a lot of trans people who have Black parents will relate to my experience. Often, their upbringing creates a barrier in the way they understand and connect with the trans community. More recently, I've reflected and wondered if I could have been more gentle with him. I was so focused on my transition that I hadn't stopped to consider that I was asking those closest to me to transition too. They needed to change some of their views and also let go of me as Kelsey and embrace me as Kenny. Papa deserved time to adjust, just as everyone else did.

I also knew that the negative feelings he held towards my transness had nothing to do with me. They were not an accurate indication of how much he loved me, in fact it was quite the opposite. Him being willing to even attempt to understand my world was a true testament of his love for me.

To the parents of kids who are 'coming out'

The term 'coming out' has become such a buzzword. I want to reframe the way we view it. When a young person comes out to you, what they are really doing is letting you in. They are trusting you with a deep, intimate part of who they are. It's a privilege.

If your child comes out to you, it's best to lean into words of affirmation and stay away from things like: 'I love you despite this' as that could make a person believe they've done something wrong. Instead try something like: 'I'm so happy that you're sharing this part of your life with me and I'm excited to learn more about you.' Or how about this: 'I feel privileged that you're trusting me with this, I'm super-proud of you for stepping into who you are.' I would also suggest that you avoid bringing in stories of other trans people you've known or had some contact with. Such as 'I knew a friend from school/work/whatever who was trans.' I understand that those statements are a loving attempt to find some small common ground. But this is an intimate moment for them to share who they are with you, so keep it focused on them.

I know from speaking to parents that one of their biggest worries is offending your child by misgendering them after they've come out. It's normal to unintentionally misgender your child, but if you shower them with love and support, that's all you can do. The slip-ups don't feel as big when you know in your heart it's a mistake. This may sound weird, but I found it heartwarming when my mum slipped up because of how sincere her apology was. She was trying and it showed. But remember, it's always best to not make a big deal out of those incidents. Bringing more attention to the situation with elaborate apologies can be more uncomfortable than the initial slip.

I want you to know that if you're a parent who is experiencing grief around their child's transition, that's normal too. You may be grieving the life you had planned for your child and the decisions you hoped they would make. My mum really struggled with this. She often cried to my sister Kizzy, because she knew she was losing a daughter. But she also knew she was gaining a son. My advice is not to shut out or shut down this grief: you need to process it in a healthy way. But do your very best not to let it come between you and interfere with your relationship with your child. In time, you will be reintroduced to a much happier person and you can build new memories with them to add to the old ones.

The Black fam

Papa wasn't the only person in my Black bloodline who was hesitant or even unaccepting of my transness. My brothers were warm and embraced me, and so was my little sister and a few of my older ones. But there are still some family members, to this day, who will only say hello to me out of pleasantries. There are some who purposely misgender me, calling me Kelsey to make a point, even though they know full well that both my mum and I requested on multiple occasions that they refer to me as Kenny. Some changed their tune as the years passed. Some of my family found it easier once I got further down the line with my transition, particularly when I started to look like a cis guy, while some only seemed to embrace me when I started getting recognition and my career began to grow. It's easy for people to put love on your name when you're seen as the little celebrity in the family. Sad but true.

As hard as I knew it would be, I had to come to terms with the idea that I would lose relationships with some family members as I became my authentic self. I have never tried and will never try to convince people, family or otherwise, that I am worthy of being loved and respected as the man I am. It stings more from the Black side of my family as I know that they know what it is to be discriminated against.

In recent years, though, statistics suggest that Black members of the trans community are increasingly being accepted by their communities, which is great news. The National Transgender Discrimination Survey published a report saying that: 'Black transgender people who were out to their families found acceptance at a higher rate than the overall sample of transgender respondents. Those respondents who were accepted by their families were much less likely to face discrimination.'[6]

Can you connect with both transness and Blackness?

Not being accepted by Papa and his side of my family made me subconsciously withdraw from my Blackness. I thought Black people were more likely to hold the same beliefs as them. Feeling shunned leaves you with a hole in your life. They had also experienced prejudice on account of their race and, to me, this put them in an even better position to understand me. That's part of why I found it so hard to overcome. Racism and transphobia, although not the same, hold many similarities. We're at a point now where any right-thinking member of society would acknowledge that racism is just wrong. Yet some people still question transphobia and even allow it. The same ideology and arguments that were used to justify racism have been repackaged to push and validate this new form of hatred, now directed to the trans community. I know this is unacceptable and I hope by the end of this chapter you'll agree with me.

Running the race

Let's start off with some simple definitions to make sure we're all on the same page here. So what is race? In short, it's just the way we categorise people. We base those categories on shared physical or social qualities, which are then put into groups. Race, much like gender, is a social construct.[7]

In pondering this reality, I knew I needed to rope in a more experienced mind than mine. Have you heard of Nova Reid? She's the anti-racism expert and TedX speaker who wrote *The Good Ally* and if you don't know her work, you should check it out. She explores the theme of race in her book and explains:

> [Race] is not real. It was born out of a race hierarchy developed primarily by Swedish botanist Carl Linnaeus in 1758 who felt the need to turn his passion from studying plants, to people. In doing so, Linnaeus outlined four key groups of humans that could be identified by colour. These were: (1) Americas (Red – Indigenous Americans), (2) Europe (White – Europeans), (3) Asia (Yellow – Asians), (4) Africa (Black – Africans).[8]

There are 400 years of history packed into what's said above, so I invite you to do your own research. There is a book called *Exterminate All the Brutes*,[9] which unpacks this history. It's also a

TV series if you'd prefer to watch instead of read.

Racism comes when we introduce a hierarchy according to these different groups. And that's exactly what happened. Nova discusses how a German scientist called Johann Friedrich Blumenbach designed a rigid race hierarchy to 'classify' humans. She said:

> He placed white (Europeans) at the top and Black (Africans) at the bottom with everyone else, all of these other 'colours', somewhere in between. What was ultimately an idea created by human and cultural bias and, in some cases, falsified tests, the notion of this race hierarchy became a prominent fixture from the eighteenth century. And it was this pseudoscience (aka lies) that created 'race' as we know it today.

Is your stomach turning? Mine too. In response to this sense of superiority, whole racial or ethnic groups can be marginalised and discriminated against. Historically this has occurred in some horrific, inhumane and cruel ways.

The next scientist to throw his hat into the race ring was Herbert Spencer. Spencer's work in identifying the evolutionary status of different humans was used as a justification of the subjugation of Black people for years. The philosopher and psychologist proposed a model called 'social Darwinism'. He basically thought that human societies were examples of different levels of evolution in humans, i.e. some were more evolved than others.[10]

His theory was based on Charles Darwin's famous book *On the Origin of Species*,[11] published in 1859. In this seminal text Darwin introduced the idea that we have evolved over the course of thousands of years through a process of natural selection. So, for the non-scientists in the room ★raises hand sheepishly★ this means that, over generations, some characteristics in a species will survive over others, which will die off. You following me? You probably are but just in case you're not, let's take a look at the example of a giraffe and its bizarrely long neck. I read in a *New Scientist* article that 'The ancestors of modern giraffes were animals similar to deer or antelope, with necks of ordinary length. However, because the trees in their habitat were tall, those giraffes with slightly longer necks had an advantage over their shorter-necked fellows.'[12] That meant the longer-necked giraffes ate more and became stronger, got on with more of the female giraffes, made more babies and eventually the only giraffes still running around were the long-necked ones because Mr Short Neck couldn't breed enough to make it through.

Now, if we move on to Spencer's social-Darwinism model, he took the same principle but applied it to the social inequalities he observed in humans. He concluded that there were 'biologically superior' humans and they should rule above the others on the grounds of this 'superiority'.

You'll be shocked to hear that this theory was welcomed with open arms by the ruling classes in Europe in the nineteenth century, who pinned themselves firmly in the 'superior' camp and started acting accordingly. According to Neil MacMaster in his book *Racism in Europe*, 'This was used to justify the stealing of land, racism, sexism, social inequalities and even concepts of eugenics'.[13] Side note: eugenics is the process of killing people with 'less desirable traits' in order to improve the population . . . this was the doctrine of the Nazis.

Spencer's research led to some doctors practising enforced sterilisation on people deemed 'unfit' for society: the poor, the disabled, the mentally ill and specific communities of colour. A disproportionate number of these individuals were Black and brown women.[14] They felt that these traits needed to be cleansed from the world. Uh huh. I think the fuck not.

Spencer was not a biologist with Darwin's credentials. He was a sociologist who misapplied the theory of evolution. Thankfully we now know it's bullshit. By the mid-1940s eugenics theories and social Darwinism had become negatively associated with the Nazi regime, while scientific consensus deemed the theories groundless.[15]

While we don't openly assign cis-het white men as superior and sterilise everyone else these days, there is a hangover from this era that continues to hold back Black communities. Studies suggest that 18 per cent of UK adults still think that some races are born less intelligent than others,[16] leading to an often unacknowledged bias that favours offering jobs or academic places to white people. Plus, given that many of our ancestors were held in slavery and not paid for their work, they wouldn't own property or have anything to leave as an inheritance for their children, while the people they were forced to serve and who benefited from their labour are far more likely to have set their children (and subsequent generations) up with property and wealth.

The amount of progress we've made to rid society of racism is questionable. And the topic becomes even more complex when we break it down into particular communities. In a lot of ways, racism in the UK isn't as overt as it used to be. And in some cases certain forms of racism that we think have 'progressed' have just transformed, flowing through the world in a way that is more distorted and undetectable, and therefore able to survive.

One thing in particular that I've noticed because of my line of work, which always feels like a throwback to a more overtly racist era, is when I see organisations plaster Black people all over their websites and advertising while they have a real diversity issue internally. Back in Georgian times (1714–76), the gentry (upper- to middle-class people) would sometimes include their enslaved Black people in their portraits as a demonstration of their wealth. Owning a Black person was the height of fashion, and they needed their assets documented on canvas in order to be on trend. Those companies that display diversity without investing in it strike me as using Black people in the same way – to be on trend.

The effects of racial discrimination on a person can be horrific. Experiencing racism is a trauma and the body activates its trauma-response system in order to cope. There are hundreds of studies demonstrating the correlation between experiences of racism with mental-health disorders. One researcher showed that American soldiers who had served on active duty showed the same brain patterns, indicating PTSD, as Black Americans.[17] Plus there's the added effects of constantly being exposed to the racist treatment of others in the news and the media. Many Black people struggle with second-hand trauma because the senselessness of the violence often leads them to fear that they could easily be next. Nova explained that during 2020, in the aftermath of George Floyd's murder, her hair started to fall out. Despite her having no personal relationship with him, the bonds of collective pain tie us together. When we see pain, we feel pain.

Studies suggest that Black men are more likely to suffer from psychosis and psychotic breakdowns[18], while Black women are more likely to experience depression and anxiety than their white counterparts.[19] This can exacerbate the different socio-economic situations of those ethnic groups. It will come as no surprise to you that someone experiencing PTSD as a result of racism, the same racism that is unresolved and still resulting in deaths all around the world today, may struggle to perform well at work. They may struggle to get out of bed. They may struggle to function at all. It's for this reason that Nova wants racism to be treated as a public-health issue. And I agree with her.

We know from studies that children are able to understand and differentiate between races around the ages of three and four.[20] This is also when they become conscious of gender. You may have seen clips of the Clark Doll test online, from back in 1951.[21] They circulate from time to time and when I see them my heart sinks a little. In the test, a group of Black children were shown four dolls, all identical apart from their colour: two were Black and two were white. The kids were then asked a series of questions in order to assess any early biases they had accumulated. These questions were things like 'Which doll is the pretty doll?' and 'Which doll is the bad doll?'

In the clips you see these sweet little kids, all smiles and chubby cheeks, consistently point out the white dolls as being 'good' and 'pretty' and the Black dolls as being 'bad'. This was back in 1950s America and my hope is that you wouldn't find the same results if the test was repeated today. But even so, this goes to prove that discrimination can take root very young.

As for me, I'm fortunate to have only been on the receiving end of racism a couple of times in my life. For most Black people, it's far more regular. In many ways, I feel like my transness acted as a protective cloak against racism. If someone was going to pick on me for something, it was more likely to be because I was a trans man than because I was Black. But when I look at the discrimination faced by trans people today, there are disturbing similarities in the way the two groups have been treated.

The parallels between race and gender

Black people have been on the front line of the queer liberation movement. The first drag queen, William Dorsey Swann, was a former enslaved person. He was also one of the first people in the modern USA to create a queer resistance group. While Marsha 'Pay it no mind' Johnson, a Black trans woman, was allegedly arrested more than one hundred times in her lifetime for her gender expression.[22] She was one of the key figures in the Stonewall riots of 1969, a series of protests that transformed the gay liberation movement. She also went on to co-found a radical activist group called Street Transvestite Action Revolutionaries (STAR). These individuals had to deal with racism and/or transphobia constantly.

Blackness and transness have a very close-knit history. When you really stop to examine it, you'll find transphobia is uncomfortably reminiscent of the racism that those around me are now so quick to condemn.

The scholar C. Riley Snorton was the first to connect them both in his award-winning book *Black on Both Sides*.[23] He discussed how Black bodies have been exploited for medical research, especially in gynaecology. J. Marion Sims, also known as the 'father of gynaecology', used enslaved Black women, without their consent or an anaesthetic (because of his racial bias that Black people didn't experience pain like white people), to develop gynaecology methods. After he 'perfected' his methods, he went on to operate on wealthy white women who were sedated. Sim's diagrams and notes contributed to the idea that white females were more 'womanly' or 'feminine' than Black females, continuing to cause damaging stereotypes.

Sojourner Truth, an activist for African-American civil rights and women's rights, delivered a powerful speech called 'Ain't I a Woman?' at the 1851 Women's Convention in Akron, Ohio,[24] which I think sums up the feeling of Black women at that time. Here's a snippet.

That man over there says that women need to be helped into carriages, and lifted over ditches, and to have the best place everywhere. Nobody ever helps me into carriages, or over mud-puddles, or gives me any best place! And ain't I a woman? Look at me!

Snorton also discussed the practice of cross-dressing in Black men in order to escape from plantations. These individuals would give up their gender identities, even if just for the time being, to avoid being caught by slave patrols. Travis Alazbanza said in their play *Burgerz*:[25] 'Black bodies have known what it means to be de-gendered, hyper-gendered and misgendered since the beginning of your slavery.' And sadly, this is true.

Racial segregation versus single-sex spaces

Separation of spaces is a discrimination tool as old as time. The Jim Crow laws were a series of anti-Black laws that enforced the use of 'coloured' and 'white-only' spaces. These came into effect after slavery was abolished, creating an extension to the suffering they had already faced. Black people, by law, could be denied access to jobs, education and public spaces such as trains, bathrooms and even swimming pools. They were also blocked from buying property or voting in elections. The ability of Black people to live well was capped in legislation. These laws ensured that Black people were second-class citizens, limiting access to spaces which white people occupied. It was all about control.

After desegregation of bathrooms in the US in 1941 on account of race, there was much pushback and people campaigned for them to be reinstated. In one factory in America, where the white employees campaigned to have their bathrooms resegregated, their gripe was just about dividing the bathrooms, not the workforce. They accepted desegregation socially (in theory at least), but the idea of peeing next to a person of colour apparently represented a step too far. It became the focus of the whole issue – and that's what I believe has happened for the trans community too.

The most prominent conversation on trans rights over the last few years is the 'protection of single-sex spaces'. The debate is so prominent that it's bordering on obsessive. Those who share anti-trans views are campaigning to force us to use the bathroom that aligns with the gender we were assigned at birth and not with how we identify today. Although trans men are a part of the debate, the real focus is on trans women as it is believed they would make women-only spaces unsafe. They believe that allowing trans women into these spaces will pose a threat to cis women.

There are a number of problems with this way of thinking. Firstly, it shows that these people don't see trans women as women otherwise we wouldn't be having the conversation in the first place. Second, it prioritises the safety of cis women and disregards the safety of trans women. Third, it assumes all people with penises are rapists. Fourth, it assumes that cis men are pretending to be women in order to sneak into toilets and attack them – something that simply doesn't happen. The basis of the debate is simply imagination and media-led hysteria.

In his book *The Transgender Exigiency: Defining Sex and Gender in the 21st Century*, Edward Schiappa explained the origins of single-sex toilets. He said:

> Sex segregated bathrooms were invented at the end of the 19th century to protect a woman's supposedly more moral and weaker constitution, a concept we now agree is sexist. But some of these claims are still upheld by the bathroom debates, assuming all people with penises are rapists and that women should be protected at all costs. All women should be protected and so should trans women and trans men, non-binary people and cis men! Sexual violence affects all genders.

Women, policymakers argued, were inherently weaker and still in need of protection from the harsh realities of the public sphere. Thus, separate facilities were introduced in nearly every aspect of society: women's reading rooms were incorporated into public libraries; separate train cars were established for women, keeping them in the back to protect them in the event of a crash; and, with the advent of indoor bathrooms that were then in the process of replacing single-person outhouses, separate loos soon followed.[26] It's sounding very similar to Jim Crow law but sold as we are 'protecting' you, isn't it? Segregation leads to discrimination.

These separate spaces were to protect cis women from aggressive men. But as I've said, most men just aren't aggressive – and if they are, then a sex-segregated toilet door isn't going to stop them.

In any case these are the people trans women need to be protected from too. We actually have a common enemy. Not only that, but the study shows cis women are also a threat to trans women. Their internalised sexism has repositioned them as the ones who also perpetuate the same norms that have made them victims.

For this, I would invite you to challenge your perspective and see the issue through a new lens. The claim is that the space protects cis women, but does it really? There is no data to prove that trans women in bathrooms are a threat to cis women. [27,28] The UN have said that the most unsafe place for a woman is her home[29] – but we still wildly force heteronormativity down our and our children's throats. Pretty much any cis woman who's been clubbing knows men who have pushed their way in to harass or even attack them. Here we are all being duped.

For me, that is the real crux of the issue. We can talk about bathrooms till we're blue in the face, but really it's just a shield anti-trans people are using to hide behind and recruit more moderate people to their agenda. The real issue here is the risk of sexual violence, which affects everyone.

In reality, evidence shows that trans people are not a threat to the safety of cis women. During the campaigning for the Gender Recognition Act reform in 2018, which allowed trans people to be legally recognised as their acquired gender rather than the one they were assigned at birth, research showed that trans women aren't more likely than cis women to sexually assault other women in women-only spaces.[30] At the time of writing this, there is nothing that suggests trans people are a threat. In fact, the opposite is true. Around 70 per cent of trans people have reported being denied entrance, assaulted or harassed while trying to use a bathroom, according to a 2013 Williams Institute report.[31]

I understand wanting to keep people safe, I want that for everyone too. What we need to remember here is that trans women are not a threat, creepy men are; cis and trans women both face a common problem The real issue here is the risk of sexual violence, which affects everyone. And the way to stop it isn't to police who goes into a toilet.

Many people see the intersection of this argument with racism too. Author Tynslei Spence-Mitchell said: 'Since the bathroom debates depend on the protection of pure [cis] womanhood at all costs, and the ideal concept of innocent womanhood in society is usually white, the bathroom debates are generally highly racially motivated, even when this is not explicit.'[32]

From my perspective, the desire to separate trans and cis people has very similar parallels to the Jim Crow laws of segregation. Keeping people divided is a tool that helps discrimination against a group of people by cutting off or limiting access to necessary elements of life. People would also look at these laws as state-level affirmation of their prejudices. By putting in place Jim Crow law, the US government legitimised biological racism, which we know is untrue and has been discredited. Implementing a bathroom law would send the message that trans people aren't who they say they are.

I think we need to take a step back and think through the position we're really putting people in if we pass a law preventing trans women from using women's bathrooms. They would have to walk into the men's rooms, which is both deeply invalidating and leaves them open to a whole new level of harassment and potentially physical assault. Plus any cis person who has the potential to be misgendered could also be shouted down and prevented from using the bathroom.

It would also set a dangerous precedent. If we allow a law like this to become reality, what's next? I don't believe it would just be bathrooms, my fear is that this would be the beginning of the end. It could catalyse the creation of more segregation laws. We can talk about bathrooms till we're blue in the face but really it's just a way for extreme anti-trans people to recruit more moderate people to their agenda, which is to segregate trans people in every area of life.

In fact, we've literally just seen this happen in the UK. The single-sex bathroom debate has been happening over the last few years, and for the most part has been unsuccessful but created much frenzy in the media. In 2021 the NHS issued guidance to say trans people may be placed on wards according to the gender they identify as. Now in 2023, those rights are being attacked. Health Secretary Steve Barclay announced at the Conservative Party conference in October 2023 that he would be launching a consultation that could revoke that rule.[33] He described it as a 'consultation on strengthening the protections in place for women'.[34] If you say so, Steve.

The basis of all of this controversy was alleged complaints from cis women. But in December 2022, Translucent, a trans advocacy group, published an investigation which involved sending Freedom of Information (FOI) requests to 102 NHS trusts, asking: 'How many natal female inpatients complained that a transgender woman inpatient was being cared for in the

woman found herself in a very peculiar situation, a combination of discrimination, with no acute terminology to explain what she was experiencing. Shortly after, Dr Crenshaw published a paper announcing her theory of intersectionality. She said that the legal system had limitations because of the law's single-use analysis when it comes to discrimination. She offered a framework that helps us understand that overlapping social identities can create multiple layers of discrimination.

Intersectionality became a buzzword in my line of work shortly after the Black Lives Matter movement gained momentum in 2020. It was becoming clear that certain types of Black people were at a significant disadvantage compared to others despite being part of the same community. Statistics from the Trans Actual Trans Lives Survey in the UK in 2021 showed that more than half of Black people and people of colour reported experiencing racism while accessing trans-specific healthcare services. And Black respondents experienced transphobia from trans-specific healthcare providers at more than double the rate of the white respondents.[42]

This is an issue close to my heart as a mixed-race, trans man. My experience of being a trans man is informed by being a Black man and I can't separate the two. My experience will never be the same as that of a white trans man: they jump over one hurdle and I've got to jump two. In our society, it's a double negative. This is soul work for me, an opportunity to claim both my Blackness and transness in equal measures and shed a light on the history of both. We need more people who are home to an intersectional identity to speak up and share our experience.

In our world of black-and-white thinking, there were some people who struggled to see me as more than one thing. I am trans. That's all they could focus on. This became even more apparent when I started working as a trans activist. If I ever wanted to speak about my Blackness in an interview, I would be shut down. They would say that we should 'focus on one point at a time'. Apparently, any hint of intersectionality would dilute my message.

How does understanding intersectionality help society?

Understanding the barriers of oppression that stop people from being able to live in the fullness of their layered identity is the first step to helping them access the life they deserve. We can all be more mindful of the intersectionality that affects different people. Every person needs a safe space where they can be seen for who they are. One of my favourite environments is when I'm celebrating UK Black Pride.[43]

The Black Pride movement is vital in recognising the unique challenges faced by Black people in the queer community. It was co-founded by Lady Phyll in 2005 and since then has grown and built up an online following of more than 100,000 people. The impact of the movement led to Lady Phyll receiving an MBE in 2016, which she turned down citing the 'ongoing colonial legacy of violence and discrimination'.[44]

For so long, Black LGBTQI+ people have languished in the margins, despite being crucial to the movement. I think the complexity of our experience makes it hard for others outside who don't share it, to bring us along with them. As white LGBTQI+ people drive forward initiatives that directly affect their lives – marriage, adoption – they do so while fighting within systems and structures that have been designed to favour their whiteness. This laser-like focus on pushing an equality agenda benefits from the disparities inherent in the system. As a result, it becomes increasingly important for us to create spaces, moments and movements that centre the experiences of Black people in the community and that prioritise our lives.

3.

Are You Going To Have THE Surgery?

Today was the day. I'd never been more excited to be jabbed by a needle. It was time to start testosterone. I had dreamed of this moment. Testosterone – also known commonly as 'T' – meant a lot more to me than physical and mental changes, it was a tool of transformation. It represented hope. This was the start of cultivating a better relationship with my body. All those years of slipping further away from myself as unwanted puberty persisted were coming to a close. We were finally moving in the right direction. This was the start of my new life, and I knew it would be glorious.

I was sitting in the waiting room at University College Hospital when the doctor called my name. I jumped up like a soldier standing to attention. Before we went into the consultant's room, they asked, 'Do you mind if a junior doctor joins our appointment today?' I turned to my mum in a silent request for her advice. She offered a reassuring smile, so I turned back and said I didn't mind.

We entered the room and no less than eight medical professionals awaited us. I instantly felt nervous. I didn't expect so many people to be there, although this wasn't unusual. I had had countless people sit in on my appointments. It was clear to me that they were trying to make the transition process smoother. I often felt interrogated, but I knew that my discomfort would serve those who transitioned after me. We discussed the potential side-effects, the highlight of which was acne. They stressed to me that the effects of T would stay with me for a lifetime. I nodded in acknowledgement and was finally sent on my way with my prescription.

Once I collected the hormones, I went to see the nurse in a room upstairs. 'Pull down your trousers and show me those butt cheeks,' she said jokily. 'First time?' I told her it was. She walked me through the process, showing me how to draw the testosterone into the needle, stressing the importance of getting rid of any bubbles and explaining how to find the right spot to inject yourself.

'Sharp scratch,' she said as she pierced my skin and then was out before I'd finished taking my deep breath. My first T shot was complete! Despite being aware that one dose wouldn't cause any major changes, I was already starting to envision a life of less dysphoria, or maybe none at all. I felt lighter picturing the peach fuzz that was about to bless my baby-smooth face. I wondered what I would look like in five years. I cried for a moment.

That was the first time in a very long time that I imagined a future for myself. What followed was years of slow but dramatic changes to my confidence and physical appearance. My voice deepened. I grew many chin hairs. My fat distribution changed, as did my muscle mass. And then there was the debut of my mini penis. (If you don't know, I'll explain what this is properly in Chapter 5.)

Starting T had some unexpected wins. People took my transition more seriously and in turn I was treated with more respect. I started to receive compliments like: 'You look good, man' or 'You've got more facial hair than me now!' The question that usually followed was: 'When are you going to have THE surgery?'

I knew what surgery they were referring to, it was bottom surgery (explained overleaf). And to be honest, at the time I didn't want it. I'd normally shy away from the conversation, saying that I hadn't thought that far ahead or that I was still considering it. I feared telling the truth. Small-minded people would never be at peace with the idea of being a man without a penis. Regardless of my answer, it struck me that the question itself is a loaded one. Surgery isn't as simple as 'Yes, I want it' and proceed forward. There are various factors to consider. And sometimes even if you do want an operation, it just isn't feasible.

There is no such thing as THE surgery

When people ask 'Have you had "the" surgery?' they are normally referring to bottom surgery, more specifically phalloplasty. This is a procedure in which trans men take a skin graft from a donor site, craft a penis out of it, and attach that to their clitoris. The surgeon would then put a prosthetic device inside the penis to ensure you can get an erection. It's normally split into three operations and the process takes between twelve and eighteen months, provided there are no complications. And yes, you can choose the length you want, although there are limitations depending on where you take your skin graft from. It's important to flag up that while this is the most common technique, not all phalloplasty surgeries are done in this way; they tend to be modified depending on the patient's needs. There are also other options like metoidioplasty, which uses just the clitoris (after it's been enlarged by testosterone) to create a smaller penis which can become erect on its own.

It all sounds very medical, doesn't it? That's because it is. So please, unless you know this person intimately, it's not a question you should be asking them. I completely understand that there is a lot of curiosity about this surgery and I don't believe people ask out of malice, but it's medical information which is personal and private so it should be treated as such. If you do end up in a situation where you ask and that person shuts you down, don't let your unsatisfied curiosity turn into feelings of entitlement.

I believe that people ask this question for a reason other than curiosity. They want to know if you've 'completed' your transition. They want to know if your body aligns with that of a cis person. Most of the trans people I know personally have no desire for bottom surgery. It can be a very complex procedure that requires a lot of resources – more on that next.

For many trans people, the 'end of transition' could be testosterone and top surgery. For trans women it could be oestrogen, feminisation and breasts. It looks different for everyone and is unique to the individual. Transitioning isn't about getting as close to a cis aesthetic as possible. Some people do aim for this, as 'passing' makes life far easier. But at their core, hormonal and surgery decisions are based on what is going to make that person happier and make them more comfortable in their skin.

I remember a comment I received on an article I had written. A middle-aged white man said: 'If you want to be a man, get a cock and balls and be done with it.' I don't know why, but I laughed. It felt like a very British thing to say. But it served as a reminder that most people only see gender through the lens of sex. When those people ask if I've had bottom surgery, it's because they are deciding how much of a man I am to them. To make matters worse, this line of thinking means that my whole identity is being assessed based on something I may never have access to.

My journey with surgery

For me, surgery was always a last resort. Not because I believe there is anything wrong with it, because I don't, but I've always wanted to make the best of what I had. I tried binding for a long time, the process of flattening your chest, before I had top surgery. Binding was never enough but it helped at the time. I was fifteen years old when I started doing it full time and I didn't do it in the best way at first. I used to buy the bandage you'd wrap around sprained knees from my local pharmacy, go home, stand in front of the only mirror we had in my house and clumsily try to wrap the bandage around my breasts and back. There were negatives to this kind of binding. Some days I'd wrap myself so tight that I struggled to fully exhale. If I was lucky, I'd get three or four uses out of the same wrap before it lost its elasticity and I had to stop wearing it because it only allowed me to take shallow breaths. But let's remember this was a very makeshift solution and if it wasn't for the lack of funds, I wouldn't have had to resort to it. There is also lots of evidence about the positives of safe binders, which is important to flag when people argue against providing them to teenagers or young people. One observational study concluded: 'Our results suggest that the positive mental-health changes associated with chest binding outweigh the negative side effects.' The researchers did, however, say that there were adverse effects in some methods and that it was important the binder found one that was safe for them.[1]

My mum got tired of watching me suffer. She saved up for weeks to buy me an official binder. Man, I was happy. It had a Velcro strip on the side so I could loosen it. I'd go to the bathroom every once in a while, and rip it off, just to appreciate a moment or two of freedom. We couldn't afford to buy more than one, so twice a week I wouldn't leave the house so I could wash it. I avoided my friends and told them I was sick or had other plans. My mum saw how sad that made me. She had always been a crafty woman; she spent most of her life creating costumes for Notting Hill Carnival. So she strutted down to a fabric shop, bought the same materials and hand-stitched me two more. That was just one of the many ways she showed me how much she loved me.

My dysphoria got worse as I grew older. It was so severe at one point that I was waking up in the middle of the night thinking, hoping, that the body I had was nothing more than a bad dream. There were times before my top surgery when I seriously considered how painful it would be to go into my kitchen, grab the surgical blades that my mum kept very safe, and use them to cut my boobs off. How many stitches could I give myself before I'd pass out? How much blood loss is too much? And if the worst came to the worst, would that result be preferable to feeling as low as I did?

Those feelings were my reality for a few years. They were real and deep. I'm far from that dark place now, but I think about those feelings every now and then. I think about how extreme they were and how either gender-affirming treatment or suicide felt like my only way out. I wish my thoughts hadn't come to that, but they did. Surgery was so necessary for me because it was a way to create a connection between my soul and physical body. Matching the visceral to the external being, me.

I'm often asked how I made decisions on surgery. No surgical option should be considered lightly. As this is such an important and difficult topic, I want to make clear: I'm not a doctor or a therapist, or anyone who is qualified to give advice for this kind of life decision. I'm simply a man who has been faced with the same conundrum, many times. I can tell you what I did but not what to do.

These are the questions I've asked myself in the past:

- Is this consuming so much of my headspace that I'm losing massive chunks of my day just thinking about it?
- If the surgery didn't give the aesthetically pleasing results I wanted but I still got the change I asked for, would that be enough for me?
- Have I tried other non-permanent options first?
- Do I truly want this for myself and have I put aside everyone else's considerations?

If I could answer yes to all of the above, I'd say I was in a confident position to move forward.

I also did as much research as possible. I talked to my therapist and doctor and, most importantly, I imagined my life with the surgery. I weighed up the pros and cons. I asked myself if I could imagine this becoming my reality and if I felt empowered by the idea of it. I'm not saying this is the only way to consider surgery or any gender-affirming treatment, but this is what I lived by.

Access to surgery

If you want surgery, there are so many factors that affect trans people's ability to have it, but on the top of the list is access. The National Health Service (NHS) waiting times are at an all-time high. The waiting-list figures for the London Gender Identity Clinic (GIC) as of September 2023 show that they have 14,152 people in line for an appointment and in late 2023 they were offering first-time consultations to people who were referred in September 2018.[2,3] This is one of the clinics you need to go to if you are to be offered gender-affirming surgery through the NHS. This is just one clinic; there are NHS and private gender-identity treatment centres up and down the country with equally daunting queues.

There is the option of going private, where the waiting times are shorter but the credit-card bills are higher. My top surgery was £6,500, which is the average in the UK, and I imagine it will continue to increase for others year on year, as with the cost of everything else. This price does not include all the other medical necessities associated with the surgery like the anaesthetic and aftercare. Bottom surgery for trans men gets a LOT more expensive. The cost of metoidioplasty in the UK is about £35,000, and for phalloplasty it's between £40,000 and £70,000.[4] For trans women, though oestrogen will make them grow breasts, surgical breasts augmentation would cost between £5,000 and £8,000, though this isn't routinely available on the NHS. And for vaginoplasty, bottom surgery for trans women, it's currently around £15,000.[5]

It's not just the cost of the surgery to factor in. Can you also afford the time off to recover? Top surgery doesn't require much time off, but bottom surgery does, especially for trans men as the surgery is split into three procedures and all require healing between the operations. If you're self-employed or precariously employed, you might find you can't afford the sick leave. On the other hand, if you're more securely employed, your employer still might not be willing to allow you the time off to recover (which might also mean that your job is at risk). And that, my friends, is why there are so many GoFundMe pages from trans people desperate to raise enough to continue their transition.

The situation in the USA is just as dire. A lot of people will rely heavily on insurance to cover the majority of their surgery costs. Even if they're lucky enough to have insurance that will pay out, they're unlikely to receive full funding. If they do raise the money, though, they have to hope they don't live in one of the nineteen states that have legal restrictions on their gender-affirming care. If they are in the wrong zip code, they would also have to pay for the travel to get them somewhere with doctors who are legally allowed to perform the operation. Yikes.

Supporting loved ones

If someone you love is considering having surgery to affirm their gender, it's natural to have concerns. You want the best for them. You want them to be sure and you want them to be safe. My big sister Kizzy and I went through many of those conversations when I was looking at my options.

I'll never forget the first time we spoke about it. I was nineteen years old and sitting in the front passenger seat of her Mini Cooper Sport. She was dropping me home after dinner. I had just started testosterone and top surgery was on the horizon. She'd pleaded: 'Don't have bottom surgery.' I asked her why. Kizzy was my number-one supporter. She still is. She shares the top spot with my mum of course. I'm her only sibling, her little brother. She is the most beautiful woman you'll ever meet, inside and out. When our mum struggled with addiction, Kizzy took on the responsibility of the home and my care without a second thought. Despite having a baby of her own, Ella Jasmine, a tiny, vibrant and energetic redhead, she also took on the role of mothering me. Because she loved me. I'll forever be grateful for that (I love you, Kiz).

Kiz had done some research and watched a huge number of YouTube videos; they left her concerned about the potential complications. I was aware of them too. It's why many trans people choose not to have surgery. I've heard horror stories of trans men who have had bottom surgery and have had urethral complications. This is the tube that lets your pee leave your bladder and body. There are modifications you can make to the procedure to reduce some of the risks. For example, you can get a penis but not move the urethra, meaning you'll still have to sit to pee, which some people find important for their experience of gender euphoria. Top surgery has potential complications too, but they are less serious.

At this point, I wasn't sure if I wanted surgery, so I didn't contradict her. I just listened. When it comes to bottom surgery, I'm still not sure if I want it, but it has always had a place in my thoughts. I spoke to Kizzy recently about it, and explained that I'd started to think I may want to go ahead with it and she completely understood.

Many trans people opt to have the procedures in order to combat depression and rid themselves of dysphoria. That's exactly why I got top surgery but it's not why, at the time of writing, I want bottom surgery. Dare to walk with me a bit here. I want to move into the future . . .

I don't believe all surgical decisions should come from a place of pain and desperation. I want us to also have surgery to elevate our experience in our bodies. I'm currently considering bottom surgery for this reason. Some people may not agree with me on this one, but don't forget that cis people have gender-affirming surgeries all the time, for example the well-known 'boob job'. I want to enhance my experience of my gender. There have been some progressive surgeries that have emerged, but there's one in particular that would take me to a place of gender euphoria and I'm really considering it. It's called Vagina-Preserving Phalloplasty. In this procedure they create you a penis while still preserving the vaginal canal. Cool, right! I know it's a non-standard gender-affirming surgery, but it feels like the perfect fit for me. A large part of the reason why I didn't want traditional phalloplasty was because of the potential complications from extending the urethra. If I can have a penis but have to keep my vagina to lower my risk, then I'm happy with that trade.

Me and Kizzy haven't always agreed but she has always respected my feelings. I can't speak enough on the importance of creating a bond in which you feel seen and heard by a person. Blood may be what brought us together, but our connection is defined by the love, kindness and space she gives me. Hearing me express a desire that was in direct conflict with what she wanted wasn't easy, it never is. But that's life. You don't have to agree. Life is full of disagreements. It's about respect and autonomy. It's about seeing a decision outside of your perspective and agreeing that that may be what's best for someone else, even if you don't think so.

Not everyone wants THE surgery

Though I hope you've started to see this from my own stories shared in this chapter, it's important for me to clearly flag up something that makes perfect sense but not a lot of people realise: not every trans person wants to 'fully' transition. Some trans men want to carry children and other people are just happy with the parts they're already packing.

Ultimately, transitioning is a completely individual path

that will be a mix and match of gender-affirming treatments (if any at all) that allow a person to feel more at home in their body. We shouldn't be encouraging people to 'fully' transition. Being 'successfully' trans is not based on how close you can get to passing as cis. Cis is not the gold standard. And a trans person doesn't have to be 'passing'. The true measure of a successful transition is how happy that person is, regardless of what treatments they have undergone.

This may be seen as a controversial statement, but if I was born in a different time with a less rigid definition of what makes a man a 'man' and a woman a 'woman', maybe I wouldn't have had any surgery at all. Don't misunderstand me, I did need the surgeries I've had – they were lifesaving for me but only because of the environment I live in. My best friend Charlie Craggs reminded me of something that I think about from time to time: there is so much judgement that is given to those people who do decide to move forward with surgery. Some people think it's unnecessary and dangerous to put our bodies through surgery and I know some are concerned about the rise in trans people seeking surgery. If you are one of those people asking why surgery is necessary, then changing the limiting way we see gender in a way that makes us feel like we never needed surgery to begin with is my answer. I've seen an anti-trans organisation use the slogan 'No child is born in the wrong body' and, funnily enough, I agree with them. We are adjusting our bodies to fit into today's world, mostly because of the rigid definitions of what man/woman should look like. But right now, we don't live in a vacuum. How others relate to us and our identities is a fundamental part of our happiness as humans.

For me, and for many others, surgery is a way to align internal feelings with physical representation. In turn, people correctly see and acknowledge you as a physical expression of your soul. Above all else, we must remember that what a person chooses to do with their body is their choice. Our bodies are for us and we have the agency to do with them what we want. There should be no judgement towards a trans person for their choices, we are just trying to make our body a home.

So to answer the original question: 'Are you going to have THE surgery?' I hope you can now see why there isn't a straightforward answer. There is so much to consider but the choice a person makes is theirs. We need to be mindful not to withhold validation of someone's gender based on how little or much surgery they have had. A 'complete' transition is whatever that person deems it to be. They have arrived when they say they have arrived.

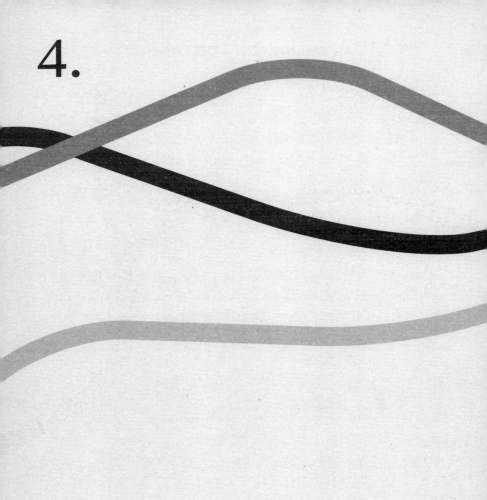

4.

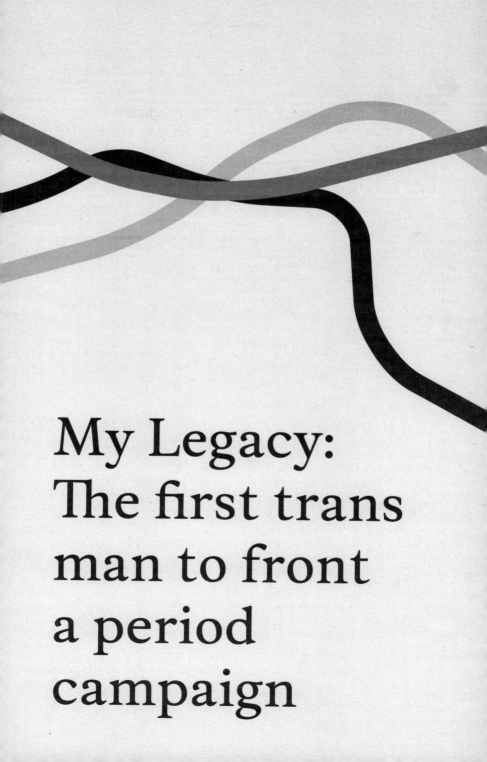

My Legacy:
The first trans
man to front
a period
campaign

Five years on the books of a modelling agency and it was fair
to say that business wasn't exactly booming. Much like their
preferred waistlines, the industry's view was narrow when it
came to who they welcomed. Let me give you an idea of what
I was up against. In London's 2019 spring/summer shows, 36
per cent of models were people of colour. Included in the mix
were sixteen trans women and non-binary models, only two of
whom were people of colour. No trans men hit the runway.
Not one.[1]

When I looked at the brands I liked best, I realised it would
be unlikely for me to work with them as they were so rigid in
what they wanted from a model. I wasn't someone they wanted
to work with because I didn't have the typical male model look.
Their minimum height expectation was 6ft while I stood at the
strong short king height of 5'5.5" – you always include the half.
I had tattoos but not *enough* tattoos. Apparently only people
completely clear or completely covered were desirable. These
fashion houses didn't deal in halfway houses.

And then there was the final, unspoken nail in the coffin.
I was trans. While they wouldn't admit it, I know some brands
would consider working with people like me a risk. They
would worry it would lose them popularity or, more
importantly, money.

Despite being part of an agency and booking the occasional
job, the label 'model' never did feel quite right. The truth was,
the work of a model didn't appeal to me. What appealed to me
was the air of confidence they'd carry with them into any room
they entered, the impact of their presence and how people
would gaze at them, thinking they were beautiful. All things I
wanted for myself.

I began to quietly quit modelling. I decided I didn't want
to keep fighting against the status quo. I dabbled in extras
work for shows like *EastEnders*, but the novelty wore off quickly.

Then there was e-commerce modelling that was equally uninteresting to me. The only job I was truly proud of and excited by was when I was invited to feature in a Pride campaign for Sky. They made a collage from a group of LGBTQ+ people's faces. I saw my slightly lop-sided smile on giant billboards alongside other inspirational people. I was representing my community. But just when I thought I should quit modelling for good, I was approached to model for something that I found far more interesting.

Model behaviour

It was January 2018 when I woke up to an email that would change the course of my life. At first glance I thought it must have been a mistake. On reading the subject line, it felt so unlikely I was the intended recipient. It said: 'Pink Parcel – I'M ON campaign.'

I hesitantly clicked it open. It was from my modelling agency. They had a job come in from a client who was doing a 'fashion-led editorial campaign' promoting period positivity. They said: 'We'd like to use a transgender model, as the client is really keen to acknowledge that it's not just people who identify as women who experience periods.'

They were right, the majority of the world did only associate periods with women and girls. Despite embodying the messaging they wanted to convey, I couldn't quite believe the invitation. The idea that a company wanted to step out of that standard script took me by surprise. Even now, at the time of writing – four years on from that campaign – only 8 per cent of period-related content acknowledges periods from a trans perspective.[2]

It's exciting to think that there's a change going on in an industry and that I would get the opportunity to be at the forefront of it, but it's terrifying too. This was the type of work

I wanted to immerse myself in. It would embrace my under-represented identity and my nuanced existence would be recognised. The campaign would face up to a taboo and make the bold statement many others were afraid to stand up and say: 'Some men have periods too.'

I didn't reply straight away. I weighed up the pros and cons, the pinnacle of adulting. I wanted to take part in the campaign but I had my concerns. I could imagine the future. A place in which anyone who bleeds feels like they can be a part of the conversation. But I could also see this campaign stirring up a lot of hate for the trans community and I would be the person they directed it at.

I knew there would be a whole new audience of people making their own judgements and assumptions about my identity. To openly say I have a womb is to say 'I am a woman' in the eyes of many people. And I was no woman. I wasn't sure if the vulnerability was right for me. I let the idea turn over in my mind and asked loved ones: 'Do you think the world is ready for this conversation?' The overwhelming response was: 'When has that ever stopped you?!' They were right. By the end of day, I had made my decision, and my decision was yes.

He shoots, he scores

A week later and I was in the studio surrounded by women, plus the addition of two men. I was hyped to see the guys. I thought they'd be joining us in the campaign. I quickly realised they were part of the camera crew. Ah well.

Photoshoots can make me feel anxious. There are so many unknowns, especially when you're working with a new team. I've had experiences where I feel welcomed and comfortable and others where I'm pretty sure they just wanted a human-sized clothing hanger. I was hoping that this one would be as inclusive as their email implied.

We got off to a great start. One of the team asked me what I wanted for lunch. Most photoshoots have a selection of beige snacks, tiny sandwiches and KitKat bars. But on this occasion, they ordered me Caribbean food: jerk chicken, rice and peas with hearty sides of plantain and coleslaw. Big day, perfect start, 12/10.

With my belly full, it was my turn to make my way onto set and the magnitude of what I was about to do hit me. I heard a voice in my head say: 'Am I actually going to speak to a stranger about my period?' Some call it stage fright, you may have heard the term 'performance anxiety', but all I know is I was suddenly scared shitless. All my pre-rehearsed lines were useless when I was hit with so much anxiety. This wasn't a normal thing to do. I didn't talk about my period. In fact, I had never done it before.

I pictured myself walking away. Announcing to the team that I needed some air and then running home the second I hit the door. I think they sensed my anxiousness. Just before going on set, the team rallied around me and gave me words of encouragement. They told me how brave they thought I was for sharing my story. Their kind words helped put me at ease and, before I knew it, 'performance Kenny' kicked in. I was ready. I positioned myself in my seat and the camera operator rolled the camera.

Let's go!

After a (sort of) painless two hours, my call time was up and I was free to go back to my normal life where no one asked me about my menstrual cycle and conversations weren't documented from three angles. I usually take time on my way home to decompress, breathe and reflect. I spent the journey home from the shoot wondering what might come of this campaign and how the world would react. Nothing could have prepared me for what came next.

We're live!

I woke up late. To be honest, I usually do. I'm a solid night owl. I do my best work at night. I rolled over to look at my phone before getting out of bed – bad habit, I know, but don't pretend we all don't once in a while! I opened the first message that caught my eye. It was from a girl I went to secondary school with who I hadn't seen in years. It said: 'I'm so proud of you for talking about this, I always knew you'd be someone special.' Don't get me wrong, that is lovely. But it was also a bit alarming, like a: 'Thinking of you today' message when you have no idea why you would need special thoughts that day. It was very kind, but I didn't have a clue why she sent it.

I scanned my mind for anything noteworthy and landed on the period campaign. They hadn't told me when it was out. It must have dropped. I scrambled around to grab my laptop to google . . . well, myself. There it was, alive and awake and living and breathing while I'd been asleep in my bed. It took one hour for my inbox and notifications to overload. My phone crashed twice and spent one particularly frantic three-minute period constantly vibrating before switching itself off. How my phone reacted was a very accurate image of how I felt.

I was on the verge of a breakdown too. As a person who enjoys retaining a level of control over a situation – or at least having an exit plan – I felt a bit helpless. Can you guess what happened next? My anxiety peaked. 'What the hell is happening?!' 'How am I meant to keep up with this?' 'I don't even know what to do with myself right now.' The thoughts came thick and fast as the communication around me mounted.

What does a smart person do when a vulnerable and potentially controversial campaign they fronted pops off? Set a Google alert for their name and the name of the campaign? Absolutely not, but that didn't stop me. Then I did what I think any considerate person would do, and checked in with my family to make sure they weren't being subjected to any trolling or abusive messages.

I then reverted back to my early, ill-advised logic. I sat down and read every comment, opinion and post. I started checking the press – and not just the friendly sites. It's fair to say those couple of days were rough. I was excited and proud of the groundbreaking campaign. But the fifteen minutes of fame had chewed me up and spat me back out again. It's not natural for us to process hundreds if not thousands of unfiltered opinions from others, especially over something as personal as a person's gender.

In some instances I faced criticism, in other moments transphobia, but mostly genuine words of encouragement. Having access to that level of feedback is wild; it's so hard not to internalise it. But the days of people keeping their opinions to themselves are long gone and that's both a good and bad thing. People are entitled to their opinions, but the internet leads them to forget to share (or in many cases not share) with kindness. I was no longer being spoken about like a person with real feelings and thoughts. I was the next hot topic on a panel show. I wasn't prepared for that level of objectification. I learned not to take things personally because if I didn't, it would seriously impact my mental health.

Most of the feedback from the campaign was positive. Plenty congratulated me on my bravery and many said they were happy that the period space was becoming more gender inclusive. But not everyone felt that way. One commenter told me: 'If you don't have bangers and mash, you aren't a man.' Those kind of senseless messages were to be expected – this is the internet after all. But what I didn't expect was the small backlash I received from people in the trans community. A few trans men were upset because I had publicly aligned our bodies with that of a 'female' anatomy.

I personally didn't feel like I had done anything wrong. It wasn't exactly breaking news that trans men are born with a vagina. But I did understand why it bothered them. Our natal anatomy has always been used as a way to invalidate our identity. If I had seen this campaign a few years back, I think I would have been upset about it too. But the truth is, my hurt would have come from my internalised transphobia. And that's why this campaign was needed.

Despite some critics, it was a massive success. There were more than two hundred articles in the press, nineteen of which were in national media, and the campaign was shortlisted for two awards. In reality, though, the campaign achieved much more than that. It prompted a change of narrative; it amplified the conversations and it sparked my career as an activist.

'It's THAT time of the month'

As part of my job as an activist, I'm invited into companies to speak about topics that affect the trans community. In one of these engagements, I took to the online stage at a prestigious woman-led organisation to speak on the subject of periods. As part of the talk, I played the 'I'M ON' period campaign video which features various facts and figures, including two that always stood out to me. The first: that more than a third of Brits will say 'I'm on' to indicate that they are on their period; and the second that 44 per cent avoid the topic when talking to friends.

When the video finished, one woman tutted and raised her hand. I welcomed her to the floor, and she screamed: 'I'm not ashamed of my period!' It's fair to say the delivery took me by surprise. Most people don't normally object with so much tenacity. I replied: 'I'm very happy for you. Whoever raised you has done a great job. But as the video said, a lot of people still feel ashamed of their period.'

As the conversation progressed, more of her colleagues began speaking about their feelings of period shame, even well into their thirties and forties. The proud-period woman still wasn't convinced. She just couldn't believe that it could be a source of embarrassment. The perspective was so far from her own that she struggled to grasp it.

Many of the women didn't like to use the terms menstruation or period, instead opting for phrases like 'shark week', 'time of the month', 'auntie flow' and others. These coded words exist in every language, which goes to show how much periods are rooted in shame all around the world. When I think about the words, to me 'menstruation' feels more formal and medical while 'period' is a social term. But 'period' is actually just a euphemism for menstruation anyway. According to Ernest Weekley's An Entymological Dictionary of Modern English: '"Period" is rooted in the Greek words "*peri*" and "*hodos*" *(periodos)*, meaning "around" and "way/path". This eventually turned into the Latin "*periodus*" meaning "recurring cycle".'[3]

The history of periods is actually far more fascinating than the history of the word. This is a back story of bizarre methodical theories. I'm not going to give you a complete potted history, but here are a few moments that to me are worthy of a mention.

Mythical dirty, sinful periods

Back in the day, like back with the ancient Greeks, they had some wild views about periods and I mean wild. They thought that when the *menarche* (first period) came late, it would have serious side-effects.[4] They also believed that blood would clot around the heart, the uterus would move around the body, and a person could descend into a suicidal depression as a result.

Pliny the Elder, a Roman naturalist who was born in AD24, believed that menstrual fluid had all sorts of mystical skills. These included withering fruit, causing insanity in dogs, dulling mirrors, rusting iron and bronze, killing bees, polluting purple fabrics (no idea why it was just the purple garms), and causing miscarriages in horses. Who knew it had so many uses?! He also believed that if a person menstruated during a solar or lunar eclipse and decided to indulge in a cheeky solar shag, it could result in death.[5]

Fast forward to medieval times and things weren't much better. Now people believed that if a penis touched period blood it would burst into flames. If you did survive the inferno to impregnate someone on their period, it was believed that child would be either possessed by the devil, deformed or . . . a redhead.[6] I called my sister Kizzy to ask her if this was the reason my niece was a redhead. She laughed and confirmed that this was not the case. At the time, the Church also refused to distribute any herbal remedies to ease the pain of menstrual cramps as they were seen as a divine punishment for Eve's original sin.[7]

Views like these persisted for longer than you would imagine. It was only in the 1950s that scientists agreed menstrual blood was not toxic and was just the same as any other blood in our bodies.[8] Even though we know our periods aren't 'dirty', we still use terms like 'sanitary pads', implying that without them we would be unsanitary. I'm pleased that we're moving away from that language and I hope that we can leave it and period shame behind.

Stigmatising people who are on their period can have dangerous consequences. According to Your Period Called, these can include 'social exclusion, economic disparity, pollution, health issues and even death'.[9] Take, for example, some rural villages in Nepal, where it's been known to exile menstruating people from the village until they have finished their period. This has led some people to die and is still practised despite being banned in 2005.[10] A charity for which I'm a very proud ambassador because of their strong stance on inclusivity and the support they provide to refugees and asylum seekers, Bloody Good Period,[11] do great workshops on this topic if you'd be interested in learning more.

Products

Before the creation of the period products we know today, the only option was rags that were used to absorb the blood. Then, when World War I left many people bruised and bloodied, medical professionals found that cellulose was an effective absorbent material for blood and used it to care for the men who managed to make it back from the battlefield. Soon nurses realised that it could be equally helpful for menstruation. This led to the creation of Kotex sanitary napkins.[12]

Mary Beatrice Davidson Kenner, a Black woman with a lot of vision, invented many of the products we use today and has the most patents of any African American woman. She invented the sanitary belt in the 1920s and patented it in 1957. A company named Sonn-Nap-Pack showed interest in buying her invention but backed out when they discovered she was Black. Kenner didn't receive any awards or formal recognition for her work. However, her inventions and contributions helped pave the way for subsequent innovations.[13]

Many other companies have joined the game since and now we have plenty of variations of these products. But even as the availability and range ramped up, we are still ashamed of using them. Until recently, vendors used blue liquid in adverts to demonstrate the absorbency of their pads. Using something that looked like actual blood was considered as rude as full-frontal nudity.[14]

My period story

I was like a lot of other teenagers – I hated my period. It was something I wanted to hide. And as I got older, that shame only grew, as it became a way for others to invalidate my identity as a man. I was fifteen when I first started my period. It felt surreal. I didn't understand why this was happening to my body.

Nobody ever had 'the period' talk with me. Most teens my age had a basic understanding of how their body worked and how to take care of it while bleeding. I was nowhere near that. People actively avoided conversations with me about bodies and how they develop, I guess out of fear that they would say the wrong thing. The small amount of knowledge I had gathered was from overhearing snippets of conversations between my sister and her friends or from some of the other girls at school.

I was in school when I had my first period. I told my teacher I wasn't feeling well and I was sent home. When I got back, my mum was worried and questioned me about what was wrong. I told her I felt a gushing feeling of fluids leaving my body, that my stomach hurt and that I wanted to go to bed. She knew what this meant. She was worried. She explained to me that I had started my period. I replied: 'A period? But Mum, I don't want to have one!'

My mum was heartbroken. She was having to explain to her son, who already suffered with gender dysphoria, that his body was going to develop in ways that weren't going to affirm his gender. I couldn't help but be sad. The start of my period was another thing in my life that didn't align with the public perception of what someone of my gender should experience. I was totally unprepared for what was happening and had no tools to manage it.

I imagine that a lot of trans teens who menstruate would struggle with what it means and how it feels. Finding studies that refer to the trans and non-binary period experience is extremely difficult as there aren't many of them. And the ones that do exist have small sample sizes, like the study of nine trans and non-binary participants who reported their first period as being an event that alerted them to the way people perceived their gender and making it a negative experience.[15] I definitely relate to this and the feeling has been echoed by the trans men I have in my life too.

It didn't help that no one ever brought up the subject with me. In fact, avoiding the topic made me feel more confused. I didn't feel like I was normal. I didn't have any trans friends I could discuss it with. I felt displaced, alone and like I was the exception to the rule. In one way I was: the rule was cisness. At the time, I only understood gender within the limited framework of being a cis man or a cis woman; I didn't know about the many layers of transness.

I wish someone had taken the time to explain to me that my journey of developing into a man would look different from that of a cis man. Maybe that sounds obvious, but without people guiding me through it, it wasn't obvious to me. It would have made a big difference to hear someone say: 'Hey, it's very normal for you to have a period and here's how to take care of your body when you have one.' Sometimes nothing needs to change to lessen dysphoria, we just want to be validated in our experience.

My periods didn't ease up. Sometimes I would be in so much physical pain, I would pass out. I could feel it in my body when I was about to come on and I'd feel distressed during the wait. It was like knowing someone was about to run you down with a car but not knowing when it was going to hit. The anticipation was miserable. When I did finally come on, I would curl myself up into a fetal position and rock back and forth gently to try and distract myself from the pain. That's how Mum would often find me in the hallway. She'd creep towards me, delicately lift my head to slip a pillow underneath and drape a blanket from her bed over my body. Then she'd sit next to me with her hand on my hip. That was her way of letting me know that she was there, and she wasn't going anywhere. Occasionally she'd try to pick me up and pull me onto her lap, but I was too big for her to carry. Instead, she'd just kiss me on my forehead and say: 'I love you, my boy.' Eventually, once the pain had subsided, I'd get up and give her a kiss on the forehead back, my way of saying *I love you too*.

It wasn't just the physical pain of periods that was distressing for me. I also didn't like the person I became when I was on my period. I was angry, mean and self-centred. When I wasn't taking my bad mood out on others, I was deeply sad. I'm sure premenstrual syndrome (PMS) played a part in why I was acting the way I was. Experiencing a bodily function that was solely associated with women and girls made me feel fractured in my identity as a man. So, although I experienced a lot of physical pain, my main issue was psychological. All I could think about was how much I wanted this thing to stop and how betrayed I felt by my body.

Even as an adult today, I still exhibit the same behaviour when I'm angry. I would rather be angry than sad – I can't do anything with sadness. Sadness makes me want to curl up in a ball and cry whilst hiding away from the world. It feels like giving up. Anger is an emotion I can use. It has power, and back then it provided me with a resistance that allowed me to move forward and to fight through on the days when the betrayal felt too painful.

When I had my period, I did my best to stay at home. It's always nicer to be in the comfort of your own bed when you're in pain. My warm sheets and soft pillows protected me from the world. Going out when you're a man on your period is a logistical nightmare. I often found myself sitting in a cubicle in the men's bathroom then realising I needed to change my pad. I'd use the wrapper from my new pad to roll up the old one, but where was I supposed to dispose of it? Men's bathrooms don't have sanitary bins. I'd be forced to carry around a used pad in my pocket or I'd have to sneak to the woman's toilets to throw it away. The disabled toilet was a second option if the door was open. But none of these were dignified solutions. More than two-thirds of masculine non-binary people and trans men reported finding managing their menstruation at home easy.[16] But in response to a question about managing menstruation in busy public bathrooms, 66 per cent of those who used the men's bathrooms felt unsafe.

I've never understood why there aren't sanitary bins in the men's bathroom. I respect that they'll be used less frequently, but, after all, the purpose of them is to maintain hygiene by creating a proper place for disposal of biohazardous waste. Having sanitary bins in the men's bathroom would benefit cis men too. Medical waste such as plasters and even nappies need to be disposed of in these bins. It's just another way that inclusivity can benefit everyone.

I was seventeen when I was approved to start puberty blockers. I had wanted to take them sooner, so this was a disappointing outcome for me, but I was just happy to have something to stop my periods and the growth of my breast tissue. I felt like everything was starting to pull together, my true destiny was unfolding. A period-free man was the man I wanted to be.

Some time later, my prescriptions were updated to testosterone, and at this transition there was a small window of spotting before my periods stopped again. This is completely normal. Like any medication, your body needs time to adjust. But I was in for a shock as, approaching my sixth year on testosterone, I started to develop phantom period pains. I was experiencing all the nasty mood swings of a period but without the bleeding. These lasted for a while and I tried to ignore it, hoping that they would disappear naturally.

I did some research, looking at forums where trans men spoke about their experiences in the hope of finding some contributions from others that had felt the same. It turns out that sometimes, if you happen to take your T later than prescribed, you may end up having a period.

Within a few months of the phantom pains starting, I began to spot again, and before I knew it I was experiencing full-blown regular pre-testosterone periods. This reawakened my dysphoria. I wasn't mentally prepared to deal with this, and these periods were physically more painful than my previous ones. I was pissed. To make matters worse, they didn't subscribe to a particular time of the month; they'd come knocking whenever they liked. Not knowing when they were going to show up meant I was always so ill-prepared and I really struggled with that.

When I stopped having periods, it gave me a chance to reconnect with my body because my dysphoria was lessened. I had made a lot of progress with embracing my body in that time, but having a period took me right back to a dark place mentally. I was much more equipped to manage those feelings, but that doesn't mean it wasn't tough.

Period shame

With the stigma around our 'dirty' periods, many people feel embarrassed about theirs. In fact, according to Always, 61 per cent of young people who menstruate feel shame around it.[15] For some, that's based on period poverty: as they can't afford products, they use their own makeshift alternatives. For others, it's the discomfort of buying period-care products. Others don't know how to use them correctly and feel they can't ask.

Growing up, I would witness the familiar stealthy interaction when one of the girls would lean over and whisper something to another. They would then do a secret handshake in order to transfer the 'contraband' and the girl would slip it up her sleeve before asking to go to the bathroom. Except a tampon isn't contraband and we shouldn't need to be so hush-hush about our bodies. I certainly felt shame around my period.

Studies suggest that almost three-quarters of people who have periods have avoided buying products when they need them because they're embarrassed to be seen shopping in the intimate hygiene aisle.[17] I was definitely in that category, but my reasons were different from most.

Shopping for period-care products would leave me filled with anxiety and paranoia. Rationally, I knew that most people wouldn't be paying attention to me picking up a box of pads, but it made me feel on edge. Some people in the world don't believe a person of my gender menstruates. Every time I went to buy products, I would be filled with fear. Fear that I was outing myself to strangers with no idea of their beliefs, understanding of trans lives and their levels of aggression. I can't tell you how many times I've dropped my pads on the counter and immediately announced (in the deepest possible voice) that they were for my girlfriend or sister. I did all I could not to raise suspicion. I played out nightmare scenarios in my head where someone would see me and shout 'That's a girl!' and I would be faced with an outburst of abuse from fellow shoppers.

I tried going to different areas to buy my period products; that way, if I was outed it was less likely to be in front of anyone I knew. I tried ordering online, but the charges for a small order made it very expensive. I could have bulk purchased but I was worried that someone might come round and see them and I would be outed once again.

I thought about how I was feeling and while many cis women carry a shame, theirs is different. There are additional complications and risks as a trans man. It's an intersectional issue. That's why I would call it 'gendered-period shame'. Once I was home with the products, this unique type of shame would only get stronger as I read the box. The labels bombarded me with gendered language about 'women' that disregarded me completely. It was bad enough that I'd had to pick up a box from the 'women's health' or 'feminine hygiene' aisle, but now to learn how to use them brought a new challenge. Maybe, to you, this sounds silly and sensitive, but it's hard to buy and use period products as a man because it constantly reinforces that you're the 'wrong' gender for the experience.

Language is important, so it was a big step in the right direction when companies decided to switch it up to more inclusive language. This certainly helped lessen my gendered-period shame. But, if we're talking about the language around menstruation, then it's the time we likely all knew was coming. We need to speak about J. K. Rowling.

The J. K. argument

I grew up surrounded by the fun, whimsical wizarding world of Harry Potter. Christmases always came with a family viewing of a Harry Potter film. I truly enjoyed the wand shop and the grand school where the students lived and studied. I, like millions from my generation, was completely captivated. But it wasn't just the fantasy of spells and Quidditch that reeled me in, it was the unlikely hero. Harry Potter wasn't the best-looking, or the smartest or the strongest. He was bullied and shunned and orphaned. But he had good friends, a lot of courage and a sense of right and wrong. It was an empowering story for anyone who felt like an outsider. I felt so inspired by the tale that one Halloween I drew that same scar on my forehead and went to school spitting spells.

But my feelings towards the story's author, and by association the stories themselves, have since changed. It was June 2020, Pride month here in the UK, but also the height of the Black Lives Matter movement's momentum sparked by the horrendous killing of George Floyd by police officers in North Carolina. It was a melting pot of emotions, because we were also all under lockdown due to the global COVID-19 pandemic. Taking to Twitter (which has since been renamed X), a media outlet had posted the link to a blog entitled: 'Opinion: Creating a more equal post-COVID-19 world for people who menstruate'. In response, J. K. Rowling tweeted: 'People who menstruate. I'm sure there used to be a word for those people. Someone help me out. Wumben? Wimpund? Woomud?'[18]

The message went out to her 14 million or so followers. My initial reaction was one of shock. Though there had been some red flags, as far as I'm concerned this comment felt blatant in its perceived lack of inclusivity. Although no one can be sure of the intention behind the tweet, as the words replayed in my mind all I could think was: 'Are you serious?' I was angry, I was disappointed. I wanted to throw all my Harry Potter books out the window.

I couldn't believe that the same woman who had written about the rise of the underdog and who had been surrounded by rumours that the much-loved Dumbledore was gay, seemed to be so at odds with the phrase 'people who menstruate'. That tweet sparked a conversation that was larger than I could imagine. Thousands of comments flooded the post, agreeing with and disagreeing with the sentiment of her tweet. As a trans man, I felt disheartened. I felt sure that hate directed towards the trans community would surely follow. The back and forth that followed this controversial tweet exposed us trans people to debates about our bodies, and often from people who didn't want to understand and had no intention of learning.

But more than this, I was personally disappointed by what her statement meant for women. From my point of view, the tweet seemed to be heavily rooted in misogyny – the hatred of women and girls. Not all women have periods. Furthermore, not all women have a womb. Not all women are able to carry a baby. That doesn't make them any less of a woman.

A woman is free to identify as such even if she doesn't have those parts or functions. That would be cruelly limiting. Linking womanhood so closely with menstruation becomes problematic when you realise how many cis women don't experience periods. There are many reasons why a cis woman may not menstruate. The main two are pregnancy and menopause, but there are also many health conditions that might cause menstruation to stop: endometriosis, polycystic ovary syndrome, hormonal medications, perimenopause, or an extremely low body-fat percentage due to illness or eating disorders. Let's not forget conditions such as Mayer-Rokitansky-Küster-Hauser syndrome (MRKH), which is characterised by being born without a vagina or uterus (or their underdevelopment). None of the women who experience these conditions are any less of a woman, and they don't deserve statements such as this one thrown at them.

For me, many of the remarks that surrounded J. K.'s tweet reminded me of the gender-exclusive language around periods when I was growing up. When we speak solely about women experiencing periods, we exclude everyone who doesn't identify as a woman from the conversation. Some may say this isn't a big deal, but I found it isolating. I didn't want to educate myself on periods as all the literature spoke about women and made me feel conflicted in my identity, so I avoided it. This in turn meant I was unable to take care of my body properly. I was an outsider, alienated in my own uncontrollable, very natural experience.

Gender-inclusive language
Rowling's argument, at least on the face of it, appeared to me to be that making space for gender inclusivity was coming at a

cost to cisgender women. I've had women approach me with the same concern and I do understand the worry. But I couldn't disagree more. I've heard statements such as 'gender-inclusive language is a step closer to erasing women'. But validating one person's identity does not invalidate another's.

I understand that women have fought for generations to gain recognition and equality. Women will always be at the heart of this conversation. I've always encouraged the use of the phrase 'women and those who bleed' as that feels like it puts women at the forefront of the conversation. Of course there are many more women than trans people who have periods, so it makes sense to centre them. But gender-inclusive language is about being just that, gender inclusive. Using phrases such as 'people who menstruate' is not meant to erase or replace women but is simply a more all-encompassing term.

For those who experience privileges based on their identity, when we start to level the playing field, making it fairer, making things more accessible, that can *feel* like a form of oppression, as if something is being taken away from you. Instead, the key here is to realise how much you and your identity take from others. Then it becomes clear that you'd be doing a disservice by not using the term.

There is an unlimited amount of space for talking about our experiences of gender. There's room to include many different perspectives, and although our experiences might not be the same, that doesn't mean they don't both belong in the conversation. The very fact that we can menstruate should automatically qualify us to talk about it as it is our lived experience. Opening the conversation enriches the subject, it's like adding more colours to the rainbow.

It's important to remember as well that periods aren't inherently female. We came to this conclusion because the majority of people who experience periods are women. But that link is an assumption, much like the many assumptions around gender that we explored in Chapter 1.

My experience of periods as a trans man is different from that of a cis woman, but they both deserve to be recognised and heard. For that, we need to have the language available. Phrases like 'people who menstruate' might seem like something to make fun of. But for me and my community, it is a small way of being reassured that we are thought of, when we've spent most of our lives not being thought of at all. If something as simple as changing the language we use has the power to make everyone feel seen and included, why wouldn't we adapt to it? And remember it's not me versus you (women) it's us versus the problem (gender equality). Our goal has always been the same. We just want the same rights as everyone else.

Companies using gender-inclusive language

In recent years, companies have clocked that gender-inclusive language benefits us all. The supermarket giant ASDA changed the name of their 'feminine hygiene' aisle to 'period products' in 2021,[19] followed closely by the UK's leading health and beauty retailer Boots in 2022.[20]

The previous language was a clear message that only women and girls experience periods. Both stores recognised that using the word 'feminine' is just a softer way of saying 'female' and made the change to be inclusive of all those who menstruate. When it comes to the word 'hygiene' – ditching that was equally overdue. Periods themselves aren't inherently unhygienic. If you don't change your period-care products as suggested on the packet, or wash yourself frequently, then you might cause yourself some problems. So make sure you have those two things covered!

This change is something to be proud of. It supports all groups and stops unhelpful and stigmatising phrasing. We're continuing to distance ourselves from the outdated attitudes of the past and refocus our attitudes to a celebration of menstruation. Game-changing moves like this one are a part of that.

Ways to release shame: talk about it

I never had a good relationship with my period. I never intended to try and build a good relationship with my period. I didn't believe it was possible. But after fronting the period campaign and doing countless interviews about it, I found myself feeling lighter. All those years of shame peeled away with each conversation. For a while I didn't understand what was happening because I didn't know how it felt to heal. And then one day I found myself on the phone to my friends, and even on the stage of panels, telling everyone that my phantom period pains were kicking my butt.

I believe we all need a little healing when it comes to our period, unless you're one of the lucky ones who had awesome parental figures who recognised periods were natural and wonderful. A lot of the shame stems from the story we were sold that then became our own. Think about that for a minute. What was the story you were told and believed about periods? That they were unhygienic? That you shouldn't speak about them? That you should hide it from others when you were 'on'?

For me, it was speaking out about my experiences and spending time in spaces, both online and physical, which were gender inclusive that helped me reframe my relationship with menstruating. Facing my period forced me to define manhood for myself, in a way that acknowledges body parts and bodily functions, but also recognises that society tends to ignore the realities of those in marginalised communities. Once I realised that I didn't need specific body parts to be a man, and a woman didn't need to have a period, I felt far more settled and even started to find the positives in having that monthly cycle.

Positives that have come from my periods

As the years went by, my relationship with my period went from unbearable to tolerable, then to accepting, and finally to the uncharted territory I never thought I'd reach: grateful. When I took a step back, I realised that I had been so focused on the negatives, I hadn't considered that there could be positives. I started to look for them and realised that experiencing periods made me a better man. I had a closer relationship with my sister because we could connect over our shared experience. I thought about how my ex-lover shed the shame she felt through our open and honest conversations. She realised that our relationship was a safe space with absolutely no judgement.

Focusing on the positives almost always inspires feelings of positivity about the topic in question, while resting in the negative can cast a dark cloud over any situation. I found that resisting my period created more pain, whereas there is so much to celebrate. For instance, if you're a person with a womb and you want to carry a child one day, a regular period is a monthly signal that that's something you may be able to do. Like any form of healing, it's quite an individual journey but you can find support along the way.

Advice to trans people or the parent/carer of trans people who have periods

I receive a lot of messages on Instagram from the parents or carers of trans teens who are concerned about them starting their period. My heart always sinks whenever I read these. It's clear from their words that they are seriously distressed at the prospect of having to deal with the potential emotional turmoil. But they are often pre-empting the worst-case scenario.

Most of those teens are on the waiting list for treatment but still have several years to go before they will be offered any medical intervention. This means, unless they can afford private healthcare, they will start their period at the onset of puberty. My heart goes out to the lovely humans that care so much and want to comfort their child in this hard time. Hopefully that young person doesn't struggle with their period at all, but in case they do, here are a few things that would have helped me growing up.

• Engage in and show us period stories from a trans perspective

For me, there is something so special about seeing another trans guy rocking it in a period-care ad or campaign. I feel proud. Seeing someone else who shares their experience may give them something to connect to. They may see themselves in that person and feel less alone.

• Introduce us to companies and products that use gender-inclusive language

The last thing you want as a trans person is to feel fractured in your identity when engaging with content, so inclusive language is so important. When it comes to the products we use, that's personal preference and a great thing to start an open conversation about. There are so many different care products available today. Pads, tampons, cups and period underwear – if you're in the market for these, I've started my own brand called Lost Fame.[21] We've designed masculine-styled period-underwear for all people with periods. There are a bunch of additional benefits to our products in comparison to our competitors and I believe we've created something really special so check it out. We even have space for a packer in one of our styles! (A packer is something that people sometimes put into their underwear to give them that bulge look.) For the sake of the planet, reusable products are preferable, but they do cost more up-front (although hopefully not in the long run). Among young trans men, pads are the most commonly used product. I'd personally suggest using period underwear as you won't see the blood and that can be a triggering sight for some.

• Don't shy away from a discussion about our period

Open conversation really changed the game for me. Being able to talk about periods with my loved ones made everything feel so normal. It was such an unlikely topic for us to bond over that the commonality feels like even more of a beautiful gift.

• Help us find an LGBTQI+-inclusive doctor if we need to discuss any issues

Being seen by a doctor who has trans patients or is queer themselves makes a world of difference. Those who have more experience with trans patients, or are part of the queer community, tend to be more sensitive with the language they use. When I see an inclusive doctor, I leave the consultation feeling seen and heard, whereas there have been times with other practitioners when I just felt small.

It's not just trans people and their loved ones who can take this into consideration, though. As an ally, you may want to financially support companies that use gender-inclusive language and products and stay away from those that don't.

5.

Masculinity
and Me

'You're more man than most men'

I'll never forget the first time someone told me that I was 'more man than most men'. I was speaking about periods at an event and one of my key points was that it was important for people of all genders, regardless of whether they bleed or not, to learn about periods. I hung around afterwards, listening to feedback and taking the conversation further with members of the audience. A young lady came up to me and said: 'I'd be so proud of you if you were my brother.' I smiled and thanked her for such a heartfelt compliment. Then she said those six words that have stuck with me ever since. If there weren't so many people around, I would have cried.

We spoke for a while longer. I asked her why she thought I was 'more man than most men' and she replied: 'The way you view being a man and masculinity is refreshing and I wish more men shared your perspective.' I instantly understood what she meant.

The version of masculinity she was witnessing was one I had spent years cultivating. The previous version of masculinity I subscribed to was not something I was proud of. So much of it was based in asserting dominance over others or making others feel small. Previously I had had a 'just suck it up' mentality and based my actions on ways that may have served men 100 years ago but not today. Over time, I noticed that not only was this a way of being detrimental to others, but to me too. It did more damage than good. I was desperate to understand and unpack it — it didn't feel like me.

Masculinity

Masculinity isn't based on any biological science — it's a reflection of the societal expectations that are put on men. It refers to roles, behaviours and attributes that are considered appropriate ways for boys and men to move in this world.[1]

I'm very conscious of reinforcing stereotypes. So, before we go deeper, I want to preface this conversation by saying that I don't necessarily believe that any trait is inherently connected with a gender. I don't subscribe to the idea that male = masculine or women = feminine. Scientifically, these constructs have little to do with our genes. How we view these two things is not set in stone because they will switch and change over time as the culture and fashions update and evolve. I believe we all hold both qualities regardless of the gender we were assigned at birth.

The earliest theory of masculinity in modern psychology believed that our gender was subject to inevitable biological forces, i.e. if you're assigned male at birth, you will therefore exhibit 'masculine' traits. These days, the extent to which your masculinity or femininity is dictated by your biology and/or your social conditioning is still a matter of debate.

I don't need to tell you the traits that the world classically associates with masculinity, but in the name of completeness we'll discuss a few. Pew Research Center conducted a qualitative test with 200 men who were asked to list some traits and characteristics that came to mind when they thought of a man who is manly or masculine. They also asked 200 women what came to mind when they thought of a woman who is womanly or feminine. Respondents associated a manly or masculine man with words that related to strength and confidence. Some commonly used words included 'assertive', 'muscular', 'confident', 'strong', 'deep voice' and 'facial hair'. The words the interviewees associated with womanly or feminine women were 'graceful', 'beautiful', 'caring' and 'nurturing', and there was also some chat about wearing make-up and dresses.[2] But these stereotypes have changed over the years.

I really dislike stereotyping behaviour because although it can help guide people to a sense of self, on the flip side it can leave people feeling less valid in their gender. At the end of the day, all that matters is that the way you act, your interests and the roles you play in society feel like you. I really wish that I could go back in time and print this on my tiny pubescent self's forehead till I got the message. But hey, maybe some of you can learn from my mistakes!

I was grateful for gender norms at one point because my deviation from them helped me get diagnosed as trans. But I hate them for what they did to my autonomy and sense of self. I'm not alone in this; a 2011 study found that 64 per cent of men under thirty-five years old think male stereotypes can do real psychological damage to people.

These notions of what makes 'a man' are so flimsy that they have changed dramatically over the course of history. Back in the day, blue was a 'girl's colour' and pink, a boy's. This was originally because pink was associated with its mother colour red, which was considered to be passionate and aggressive, so therfore male. The ancient Egyptians developed make-up for men to enhance their masculinity[3]. The fellas used black pigment to create extravagant cat-eye designs. The bold face markings signified wealth and status, and they believed that it would catch the attention of the gods Ra and Horus. Ra was the god of the sun, order, kings and the sky, and Horus was god of kingship, healing, protection, the sun and the sky. To be fair, the sun and the sky are big remits so it does seem sensible to job-share. But the ancient Egyptians weren't the only men to apply cosmetics.; the ancient Greeks and Romans often applied rouge to colour their cheeks and they painted their faces with powders of ground-up minerals. They even used a DIY nail polish of pig's fat and blood. Nice idea, but I think I'll stick to Fenty.

High heels didn't start off as the figure-enhancing female footwear they are today either. They were first worn in Iran in the tenth century. Wealthy Persian men wore them when riding horses. The heels clicked into the stirrups and helped the rider secure his balance so he could shoot his bow and arrow more effectively. These men then started wearing them when not on horseback as a handy way of enhancing their height. It was only when women started toying with incorporating elements of men's fashion into their own that they took ownership of the high heels. By 1740, men (other than perhaps Tom Cruise) had stopped wearing them altogether.[4]

As masculinity is subject to change, it probably won't surprise you to learn that it differs greatly depending on a person's race, educational background and their age. Black men are more likely than white men to describe themselves as very masculine, and the same pattern holds for women. About half of Black men (49 per cent) and Black women (47 per cent) would say they are very masculine or very feminine respectively. But in white groups, only 28 per cent men would say they are very masculine and 27 per cent of white women would say that they are very feminine.[5]

Interestingly, it seems parents are more protective of their sons' masculinity than of their daughters' femininity. A group of researchers found that most adults were open to the idea of exposing young girls and boys to toys and activities that were typically associated with the opposite gender. But only 64 per cent said it would be a good thing for parents of young boys to encourage them to play with toys or participate in activities usually thought of as being for girls, whereas 76 per cent thought it would be a good idea for girls to play with boys' toys.[6] So, do we value masculinity more? Or are the consequences of deviating from gender norms more serious for men in our society than for women?

Me and manliness

Before coming out as trans, I had a lot of interests that society would usually categorise as 'feminine'. I adored music made by female artists. I felt like they plunged to the depths of my soul with their lyrics that really resonated with me. In the privacy of my own home, I'd bang out songs by Cassie, Beyoncé, Fergie, Britney Spears, Jordin Sparks, Kelly Rowland, Taylor Swift, Sugababes and the Spice Girls. It wasn't uncommon to see – or hear, more like – my mum and me singing our hearts out to Atomic Kitten at karaoke. Good times.

I started gymnastics when I was eight years old and continued until my mid-teens. It's traditionally a female-dominated sport. Thankfully, as some men did compete, I felt I could hold onto it. But I wasn't raving about it to my friends and, eventually, I swapped gymnastics for weightlifting because it felt more 'masculine'.

The world saw me as a girl, so, to them, my interest in gymnastics was a natural fit. But once I became Kenny, I felt the pressure to be more masculine gradually mount up on me. Being expected to act in a 'masculine' way to prove that I was a boy is absurd, but like many boys, both cis and trans, I felt obliged to obey this stereotype until I felt I fitted the bill.

I catapulted myself into anything and everything widely considered masculine and cut ties with all of my 'feminine' interests, which meant suppressing the hell out of my urge to sing along to the Sugababes' 'About You Now'. It was uncomfortable. I didn't want to let go of those 'classically feminine' hobbies, but I was worried that others would judge me if I didn't. I believed that if I didn't act masculine, I wasn't a man. The two felt inseparable and it caused huge tension in my relationship with masculinity. I felt I had something to prove as I wasn't assigned as a boy at birth. It was a shame. I was investing so much of my energy into 'making up' for something, but I didn't have to because I was already man enough. The pressures were silencing, forcing me to become a version of myself that wasn't complete. The wildest thing was, I had just escaped the captivity of a false identity to walk into this new type of cage.

My close guy friends, Andrew, Shaq and Nicholas, were really accepting of me. They were sensitive to my trans-related triggers and did their best to support me. But at one point I felt resentment towards them. My feelings of not being enough were exacerbated by the differences in our experiences of puberty. Mentally we were on a similar path, but our bodies were becoming less and less alike. They were growing tall and popping out peach fuzz while I was developing undesired boobies and hips. Not fun. Some may find the word 'boobies' a unique choice of words but it's a deliberate one. When I was younger, my mum realised that the word 'breasts' would trigger my dysphoria and so, with her Scouse accent, she said 'boobies' instead. Something about it felt less intrusive; it was a much softer and cuter way of labelling a body part I'd rather forget I had.

As that gap in our physical appearances got bigger, people questioned my gender more and more. This did nothing to help my 'not man enough' feelings. At the best of times, I could pass for a pre-pubescent or early teenage boy. But as we got older, that whole 'my puberty just hasn't hit yet' excuse stopped working.

Hypermasculinity

To compensate for my lack of male physical appearance, I fell into hypermasculinity. I thought if I recreated the behaviour I had seen boys encouraged towards, there would be fewer questions about my gender. Spoiler: it didn't work out as I had hoped.

Hypermasculinity is a term for the exaggeration of stereotypically male behaviour. This could be an emphasis on physical strength, aggression and sexuality. Basically, if you're watching a 1990s film and they describe someone as 'macho', you're looking at someone 'hypermasculine'.[7]

I hit the gym, started putting on a deeper voice and forced

myself to be emotionally 'harder'. I stopped hugging my mum. I stopped crying. I allowed myself to get angry, I egged myself on and didn't have any control of my emotions. For a very, very short and highly embarrassing period, I glued on facial hair. I don't want to hear any questions about where I got the hair from – mind your own business! From afar it didn't look terrible, but up close it was far from convincing. The longer I wore it, the more the glue would peel. When it got too bad, I'd just rip the whole thing off. Andrew, who knew it was a fake moustache, would joke, asking when I found the time to shave halfway through the day! I probably looked more like a drag king than a trans man. But I was determined to find ways to look more manly. If there are any trans men or masculine-presenting non-binary people who are thinking of trying out a DIY beard, please don't. Feel my second-hand embarrassment. Using an eyebrow pencil to darken your facial hair is a much more effective tactic. Trust me.

Hypermasculinity didn't do anything for me other than make me feel like someone I wasn't. All this pretending to be a macho man was distancing me from who I truly was. It pulled me towards friendships I shouldn't have invested in. I refused to indulge in the enjoyment of my childhood activities. I continued to suppress anything I deemed to be feminine until my mid-twenties. This type of masculinity had me in a real chokehold, but ultimately I felt betrayed by it.

Toxic masculinity

Hypermasculinity was a stone's throw away from what is now commonly known at 'toxic masculinity'. Although I never fell completely into that world, for a short time I did come dangerously close. I'm grateful to my mum for the moral compass she provided me with that kept me from going down completely the wrong path. She was my north star; she raised me to have a strong sense of right and wrong. I sometimes struggled to distinguish if something was completely right, but I always felt it in my gut when something was completely wrong.

Toxic masculinity is similar to hypermasculinity in that it's when a person is exhibiting the stereotypical 'man' traits. But with toxic masculinity the behaviour has a negative impact on men and society as a whole.[8] For example, a man who thinks physical strength is important and goes around entering weightlifting competitions to demonstrate his muscles could be seen as hypermasculine because that has no negative impact on others, while a man who thinks physical strength is important and goes around starting fights to demonstrate his muscularity is showing toxic masculinity. That's a very basic example, but I hope it helps you get your head around the difference between these two forms of too often hyped-up masculinity.

Many men feel the need to conform in toxically masculine spaces. I'm sure it's partly because they want to be accepted by the boys. Particularly when we're young, we'll go to great lengths to be accepted by our peers. Toxic masculinity quickly spreads like a disease through a group of men, infecting them. It takes hard work to decontaminate those it touches.

My extended friendship group included the boys that lived near me. They would hang out in blocks in my area or in pubs on my local high road. Some of them were not nice boys. Hanging out with them just didn't sit right, something stirred in my gut, my spidey senses would tingle. I never felt safe. Their parents would brush off their bad behaviour with the old classic: 'Boys will be boys.'

I won't lie, hanging around them made me act in ways I'm not proud of. I perpetuated some of the unkind behaviours that I am now so adamant that men should let go of. I laughed at jokes about women being on their period and sat and watched while they chatted up women, never taking no for an answer.

Just because I was socialised as a girl, and considered by many to be a girl at this time, didn't mean I was beyond being sucked into wanting their approval.

Addiction treatment centre Green Hill Recovery explained about the far-reaching impacts of toxic masculinity. They said: 'It can lead to more violence against women, as men may feel entitled or validated in their abusive behaviour. Unhealthy masculnity is also incredibly detrimental to men. Research has shown that men who display traits of toxic masculinity are more likely to experience isolation, poor health, and unhappiness.'[9] Men with toxic traits tend to suppress their emotions, and this has the potential to create emotional distance in their replationships. Men who struggle to express their feelings can come across as detached, and this leaves their partners feeling unsupported and unloved.[10] Men with toxic traits are more likely to experience anxiety, depression and an unhealthy relationship with drugs and alcohol. They're more likely to engage in risky behaviours and are statistically more likely to die by suicide.[11]

For most men, toxic masculinity drags them away from the people they truly are. It blocks their growth and restricts them. Personally, I view toxic masculinity as immaturity. If a person hasn't found a way to feel powerful within themselves, they make others feel small instead. It's not true power. True power doesn't make others feel weak. Healthy masculinity is maturity. It's self-assuredness and a feeling of comfort in a person's identity. That's not to say they don't have wounds and areas they're working through, but it means that they are aware of their faults and challenges and don't shy away from them.

In my life, I got to a point of reckoning when I knew I was going wrong and had to make a change. One day I woke up and said, 'Fuck it!' and took a leap of faith. I realised I had nothing to lose by letting go of those negative traits and everything to gain. I was ready to get to know the man I was becoming without tripping him up with stereotypes and insecure competition. That's when I started on a new journey, one that fulfilled that yearning inside me for a healthy masculinity that didn't negatively impact others around me.

Healthy masculinity

You'll be pleased to hear that I now have a great relationship with masculinity; we're going steady and enjoying the ride. It mattered to me to heal how I related to 'manliness' before I had any gender-affirming treatment. I didn't want to make such important decisions from a place of not feeling like I was enough.

A lot of trans people I speak to will say that once they started their transition, they constantly had to re-evaluate their sense of masculinity and femininity. It's not a one-time fix. It's something you assess and act upon and then course-correct if you find you're on the wrong track. Then you start the process all over again. This is especially important if you're seeking gender-affirming treatment and undergoing physical changes.

For me, as I started to feel more comfortable within my body, I began to shed layers of masculinity I didn't need any more. Soon enough, I started stepping into more of a divine masculine energy and I've been really happy with the man I am ever since. Ironically, I found a great balance in my masculinity when I reintroduced some of the traits I had been taught when I was socialised as a girl.

The first step in that journey was to ask myself better questions. The first being 'What kind of man do I want to be?' If I didn't know what my goal was, how could I start to work towards it? I sat down with my journal and wrote out a list of the traits I most prized. I want to share that with you in case it is helpful in navigating your own journey with masculinity or femininity, or helping someone you love to do the same:

I want to be the type of man who . . .

. . . makes people feel safe
. . . people can trust
. . . keeps to his word
. . . lives by his morals
. . . lives with integrity
. . . holds himself accountable
. . . is self-assured
. . . knows his worth and value
. . . can protect those he loves physically and financially
. . . looks in the mirror and likes the guy looking back at him
. . . his partner is proud of.

Healthy masculine is much bigger than the things listed above, but this was where I started. These are not things that we're necessarily born with. Some of us are taught these qualities and some aren't, but it's never too late to learn. It's never too late to better yourself. It's never too late to start taking care of ourselves.

In time, I developed five key pillars that I felt meant I was moving in the right direction to being the man I wanted to be. These became the touchpoints that helped me cultivate healthy masculinity. I can't say I do all these things perfectly, but when I make an effort in these areas, I am able to hold my head up high. They're not just things men should engage with; these would benefit people of all genders, but as we're talking about healthy masculinity I've made that my focus below.

1. Role models

Men lack good role models and we all need them. I believe if I'd had someone healthy coming alongside me and speaking into my life, it would have stopped me going down the wrong path with those kids from my area. Having someone who is a few steps ahead of you who you can look up to is such a great way to become a better man. For me, I wanted to learn from men who subscribed to healthy masculinity and having those people around is a shortcut to success.

The people I admire and benefit from most are the ones who have experienced their own trials – although they don't have to be identical – and have grown as a person off the back of it. I make sure I ask those people questions, and that I actively listen to their answers. I know that, if I can understand not just what they do but the thought process behind it, then I'm onto a winner.

You don't need just one mentor. I've found that surrounding myself with a number of wise people from different walks of life and backgrounds has built me up as a person. As a man, I don't feel the need to only be led by men. In fact, I think a woman mentoring a man can add huge value to his life, and maybe even protect against any tendencies towards toxic masculinity.

2. Emotional literacy

Boy oh boy! This, right here, is a game changer. Emotional literacy could be a whole book in itself – in fact, there are hundreds already out there on the market today: *Why Has Nobody Told Me This Before?* by Dr Julie Smith[12] and *How to Do the Work* by Dr Nicole LePera,[13] to name but two. I can't claim to be as experienced as the authors of those books, but I have picked up a few things along the way that have massively helped me in my own journey.

When I speak about emotional literacy, what I mean is the ability to express how you're feeling to those around you.[14] I believe that if you can't name what you're feeling, you'll be trapped inside it. Poor communication makes it much harder for those around you to meet your emotional needs – they're not mind readers. While that can affect all your relationships, it's likely to impact your romantic relationship most.

There are plenty of people who like the idea of it, but breaking a pattern of squashing down your emotions can feel like a daunting task. I use the Feelings Wheel.[15] Google it if you're not sure what I'm talking about. It's a great tool for taking you step by step through how you're feeling to work out exactly which words to put to it. Struggling to define and understand how you're feeling can mean those emotions come out as anger and frustration instead. And that's no good for anyone. Even though I've been working on this stuff in myself for a while, I'll still look it up from time to time. Don't judge me – there's nothing wrong with a cheeky cheat sheet!

Another helpful tool is therapy. A shout out to my own therapist, Niki! Therapy was a compulsory part of my transition process, but later in life I made the choice to go back. Therapy taught me to trust another person with my emotions and gave me a framework for healthy communication. A surprising side-effect from this has been that not only has my relationship with myself improved, but also my relationship with the women in my life. My being able to access and understand my emotions has created safe spaces for them to share with me.

All of these practices helped me to strengthen my tolerance for distress and that is key when it comes to managing emotional distress. Those who haven't developed this skill can at times go through an emotional incident and make it worse. They tend to become overwhelmed by stressful situations and may sometimes turn to unhealthy or even destructive ways of coping.[16]

As a man, it is especially important that you learn how to release emotions healthily. Now that's not to say they won't come up again because they probably will. But you need to have a framework that you follow, so you don't need to blindly work out what to do in a stressful situation. You already have a plan in place and you just have to follow it. If more men were on top of this, we would have far less violence in the world.

In most instances, I know that if I feel angry, I can probably trace it back to feeling hurt because someone has crossed my boundaries. What hides behind it is sadness but rather than accept that and let myself feel it, I find it easier to be angry.

I had to put the work in to build resilience. I had to learn to ask myself why I was feeling this way. I had to learn to sit with what made me upset. I had to learn to grieve losses without letting the absence of that thing or person consume me.

Practically, aside from the introspection, therapy and the trusty Feelings Wheel, there are a few other things that I find helpful. When I am grieving the loss of a person, I do something to keep their memory alive, like tell a story or visit a place we went to together. When I feel like I can't name how I'm feeling, I meditate and try not to get too lost in my own head. When I feel like everyone's trying to piss me off, I get a good night's sleep before I act on it – you'd be surprised how different you feel when you're not tired. If what I feel is pure rage, I take myself away from that person and head straight to the gym. Moving my body helps me to channel that tension into something good.

I hope these simple suggestions help, but I don't want to run the risk of causing you more damage by not pointing out the obvious: if you're in a bad place with anger or feel emotionally overwhelmed, please speak to a professional. I'm on your side and so are they. A doctor, therapist or even an emotional-health charity like Mind will help you work out where you're at and what you need. It may feel unnatural and painful to speak to someone else, but it could do you the world of good.

3. Fitness

Investing in my physical health was one of the best things I ever did. The mental and physical health benefits are too numerous for my little fingers to type out. As I said, when processing emotions gets tough, fitness provides a healthy outlet. For that reason, I'm very grateful for the gym.

Training and working towards a strength or fitness goal has done far more for me than just tone my body. It's taught me discipline. It's taught me mental restraint. It's taught me not to give up because something is hard. It's improved my relationship with my body. It's helped me to talk about my emotions more. It's helped me work through my thoughts. It's built my confidence.

I joined a gymnastics group when I was eight years old and continued to go till my late teens. By then, my interest in fitness and sports had shifted to bodybuilding. A family friend took me to the famous Gold's gym – their slogan is 'The Original Home of Serious Training' and they started in Venice (or Muscle) Beach. The noise of weights slamming against floorboards was like music to my ears. I instantly knew this would be my second home. I watched as ripped guys lifted weights that were three times heavier than me and I was in awe. I thought I was relatively strong from my gymnastics training, as it requires a lot of core strength, but I soon realised I was wrong. When I sat my puny ass on that bench press, I struggled to lift 30kg. I decided I wanted to work my way up – I can lift over 100kg now! I've been going to the gym ever since.

Don't get me wrong, there are many ways in which a gym – particularly one like that – can lead to toxic masculinity. I'd see men trying to prove how 'manly' they were by attempting to push a weight that was well beyond their limits. If I'm totally honest with you guys, and you know I always am, I wouldn't say my initial reasons for getting into weightlifting came from the right place. But over time it's shifted to a much healthier dynamic.

Seeing progress in my abilities was key to keeping me engaged with training. As my body changed through weightlifting, it also helped me move away from a more traditional female figure. For me, that was gender-affirming and an encouragement. But to make sure I was consistent, I couldn't just rely on my will power. I had to make sure that I was engaged with my goals and, let's be real, that the gym wasn't too far away from my house, otherwise I would never have trekked there.

4. Bromance

I love a bromance. I think it's the best type of healthy masculinity. This year I joined a beautiful self-development programme for men hosted by Jordan Candlish.[17] The course lasted twelve weeks and we worked on a different area of our lives each week. The purpose of the course was to hold space for one another. It was to allow men, who often don't have a healthy outlet for speaking about how they're feeling, to share and grow on a journey of self-improvement. The most important thing about the programme was that the men were there to support each other.

Hearing the thoughts and fears of others allowed me to build empathy and see the world in new ways. Some of the men on the course shared traumatic stories, and in many cases it was the first time they had said how they felt out loud. But in the next breath they would gloss over it and dismiss those experiences as minor. On one occasion I asked if I could have the floor to respond. I simply said: 'What you've been through is traumatic, messed up and unfair. I'm sorry you've had to experience that. If you ever need someone to talk to about it, I'm here.'

The man who had spoken to me got teary-eyed. All that most of us need is a simple 'I see you and your burdens'. It can make all the difference. I wanted him to feel it, then let it go and know that he didn't have to go through that process alone. Men need to have spaces like these in which their pain is acknowledged. The number-one killer of men under fifty years old is suicide.[18] Creating room for compassionate conversation is vital for a person's health and, in some cases, their survival.

5. Haircare

I can't tell you how proud I am of my beard. I've literally made stories on Instagram purely dedicated to showing it off. I waited years to have a gorgeous plumage on my chin and you better believe I'm going to take good care of it. I've got a stronger beard than most cis men . . . just saying. I trim my facial hair every three or four days. For me, it is an act of self-care. Taking pride in my appearance is vital for my relationship with myself.

I'm not saying you have to grow a beard – what would be the point when you can't beat mine anyway?! But jokes aside, there are aspects of your body, appearance and style that you can invest in. And it will feel good to do so.

My journey with masculinity and femininity has been one of unlearning and relearning and I've found (and am *still* finding) a beautiful blend of traits that have typically been associated with each. I encourage you to allow yourself the time to discover your own unique blend of characteristics, free from the bounds of a binary understanding of gender.

6.

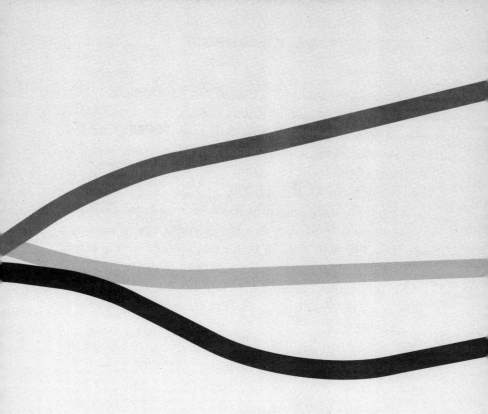

Mini Penis!

Sex was the first way I really started to explore my body. The growth of my boobies and the start of my period were my first nudge to do this. But given how they made me feel, I decided to opt out. At the beginning of my sex life, sex really served as a reminder of the bad relationship I had with my body. And in most cases triggered my dysphoria.

As painfully triggering as it could be, wonderful sensations such as orgasms proved to me that I could enjoy my body. Since then, I've built a much better relationship with not only sex, but also with my body and the fluidity of my sexuality.

One of the most common questions I'm asked by cis people is: how can I help my trans partner to be more comfortable in the bedroom?

I've always struggled to answer this question because it's not just about sex. Creating a better relationship with sex requires a much more holistic approach that looks at your relationship with your body, your sexual turn-ons and offs, how much you know about your sexuality and how you feel about it. I'm sure there are others, but these have been key in my life and they relate to people of all genders. So although this chapter will answer the question above, I'm also hoping as a cis person you may learn more about yourself while discovering that answer.

The start of my sex life – before men

Up until I was twenty-one years old, I identified as straight. My attraction to women was always obvious to me. I find their minds highly intriguing. I loved their curves – I'm a big boobies man! The softness of their touch, their passion and their loving nature, I felt their love pour into me. But I would be lying if I didn't say that I defaulted to thinking I found women attractive anyway because in our society heterosexual relationships are the norm.

Dysphoria

I started having sex in my mid-teens. I did enjoy sex with women but my dysphoria was there, running rampant, at the beginning of my sex life. I was OK with having a vagina when it was private. I didn't love it, but I didn't hate it. But when it had to get involved with someone else, I'd be like 'Hell, no'. I primarily focused on my partner's pleasure to avoid being touched myself. I wanted to be touched too, but it was just so difficult.

I felt pulled in different directions. My hormones were telling me to get stuck into sex. I enjoyed some of the physical sensations. But on the other hand I was in such mental discomfort that my head would override any pleasure my body was feeling. My self-consciousness stole the energy I could have been investing in the experience with that person. In some cases, I was going through the motions of having sex for my partner, not because I wanted to.

To be clear, none of my partners ever forced me into doing anything I didn't want. But I couldn't help but feel an obligation to be sexually active with them. Everyone else was having sex, so why shouldn't I? I believed that 'real men' had lots of sex. I thought it would reinforce my masculine identity. I also wanted to experience the deepening of intimacy and connection that getting physical can bring between two people.

I found it really difficult to navigate having sex. Like, what do I even do? Nobody provided me with sex education and those closest to me avoided the discussion, so I didn't have a clue what I was doing. That's pretty normal for an experimenting teen, but I had no idea what pleasure was supposed to look like for me, or how to go about it in a gender-affirming way. What was most sad was that there was absolutely no one I could ask.

Rhino

Then along came Rhino. Quickly after being gifted him, I wouldn't have sex with others without using him, my strap-on. Yes, he has a name. He's a slightly-too-light-for-my-skin-colour, six-and-a-half-inch extension of me – didn't I tell you to never forget the half? Rhino was such a prominent part of my sex life that he started to feel like a part of me – but in reality he wasn't. Over time I slipped into an unhealthy attachment. I felt that I was unable to offer 'real' pleasure to my sexual partners without him. While I know some people find prosthetics gender-affirming, for me using Rhino over time left me feeling less connected with my partners as I was having sex with them without using a part of my actual body. At the time I believed that penetrative sex was the core feature of a sexual interaction, the rest was just a warm-up act before the main event. But this attitude would cause me problems later.

Initially, Rhino made me feel safe. Sex for me was an exercise in imagination. Watching Rhino go in and out as moans of pleasure fell on my ears was stimulating for me. I would imagine the feeling of a warm vagina passage caressing my dick. This, paired with some physical touch like grabbing a woman by the hips and thrusting my waist against her whilst I bit her back lightly, was enough to make me orgasm.

My vagina, on its own, did not make me feel dysphoric. But when it came to sex, the non-presence of a dick did. Not having my own six-and-a-half inches to push inside of my partner made me feel like something was missing. The best word I can find to describe what I was feeling is 'desiderium'. It means a feeling of longing or, in some cases, a feeling of loss. This was a new feeling for me; a new strand of gender dysphoria that I hadn't previously experienced.

For a long time, using Rhino helped me alleviate some of my dysphoria – we'll touch on other ways I managed to do this later. He helped me bridge the gap that I felt was missing. But the time had come to let go.

As I got older and more comfortable with my body, I found myself needing more sensation. As much as Rhino and I were attached, he left me feeling detached from the mutual pleasure I was supposed to be experiencing. I wanted to use more of my body. I needed more body-to-body contact. I needed more touching, sucking, biting. So much of my joy and pleasure was reduced because of my gender dysphoria, but now that I was healing from that, I found myself yearning for more connection in every aspect of life. Especially sex. After years of disconnection, I wanted a fucking sensory overload, and I deserved one.

I switched things up. I put Rhino back in the drawer and decided to try and face it alone – without my crutch on my crotch. It was incredibly hard at first. I was forced to be more creative and to play around with pleasure.

My Rhino days were fun, but he ended up in temporary retirement when my whole sex life was blown open because I started exploring men. Strap in (pun intended), it's gonna be a ride!

Fuck, I've got to come out again

I always had an inkling that I found men attractive, but I never acted on it. When I was younger, I found it hard to differentiate between admiration for a man's appearance because I wanted to look like him and an actual attraction (i.e. wanting to rip his clothes off). But even if I had decided to explore it, the boys that were showing an interest in me were straight and I was leaning more into my Kenny identity, so what was the point? Even with that niggling feeling that I was drawn to men as well, I was too afraid to explore it. Like most men, I equated my masculinity to being straight.

In the summer of 2016, I finally acted on my interest. The previous year I had suffered huge grief, the type that makes you realise that life is short. In that moment, the idea of exploring men felt like nothing in the grand scheme of life. I had no fucks left to give. Both of my parents had just died, and I was left with more responsibility than I could handle. I had a two-bedroom flat near central London, three dogs to look after, a motorbike and car to pay for, all with no income. I was fucked. Not only that, but I had funerals to coordinate and pay for, while processing the loss of the two most important people in my life. I was broken.

Naturally, the stress of my whole situation was getting to me. I needed a break from the seriousness of adulting. Not only that, but I had become sick of the pity people would show me. Everyone around me looked at me and just saw the kid who had lost both his parents, nothing else. I couldn't escape the feeling of the loss because it was all everyone spoke to me about. I wanted a clean slate, even if it was temporary. So, after finalising Papa's funeral plans, I asked my sister Kizzy to look after the dogs and I ran off to Houston, Texas. I had always wanted to go to America, it spoke to the entrepreneur in me, it was the land of dreams after all. Houston wasn't my first choice, that would have been NYC or LA, but I had been speaking to a guy called B who lived out there, and I figured it would be nice to have a friend show me the city.

You know when you arrive in a new country, make it to the doors of the airport and that first wave of warm air hits you? All I could think was: *I could be anyone I wanted to be here.* Freedom and healing was what I was seeking. I still felt the emotional weight of my loss, but H-town was like a new beginning. I struggled while I was out there. On one of my harder days, B found me cradling myself in tears in his walk-in wardrobe. On occasion, I'd push the accelerator in my BMW M4 a little too hard because speeding felt freeing. Looking back, I can see that this isn't advisable behaviour, but at the time it felt pretty normal when grieving such tremendous loss.

After spending a few days around B, I was taken back to those same feelings I had as a teen. Is it attraction? He liked me, or at least his friends told me he did. One evening, I decided I'd shoot my shot. We kissed on that day, and it gave me the much-needed clarity I was looking for. I was indeed attracted to men.

It's not uncommon for a trans person's sexuality to change. A survey of trans men who'd started transitioning (including hormones and/or surgery), showed that 40 per cent reported some shift in sexual attractions.[1] The same results were found in a 2005 study of 232 American trans women who had transitioned.[2] In that study, 43 per cent reported significant shifts in their sexual orientation. There's no scientific explanation as to why this happens, but in my case it's because I finally started to feel at home within my body and so I felt free to explore. At the time of meeting B, I was pretty much passing consistently and had started to feel like myself.

Coming to the realisation that I was bisexual was exhilarating, but it brought up a new world of feelings I had to unravel. I was excited to explore men. Having a whole new body type to play with sounded like a great time. But I was worried about having to come out again, for the second time. My friends were smart enough to know the difference, but a lot of people didn't understand the difference between gender identity and sexual orientation, so they'd conflate the two, often asking 'Well, why did you transition just to date men?' Just to clarify, gender identity is different from sexual orientation. Gender identity reflects a deeply felt and experienced sense of one's own gender.[3] And sexual orientation refers to a person's physical, romantic and/or emotional attraction towards other people.[4]

Letting go of being straight

Liking men put me in emotional turmoil. Saying goodbye to being straight was challenging. I was afraid of losing that part of myself. I believed that being straight meant you were more masculine – thank God I know that's not true now. But it really put a strain on my existing relationship with my gender. Embracing this shift in my sexuality had me feeling so disconnected from my masculinity that it fucked with how I felt about myself. Because of this, I didn't feel connected to my gender and for a while, I felt lost.

My romantic attraction to men was already affecting my sense of self. But these feelings were exacerbated by the sex I was having with men. I had so much to unpack about sex. Physically exploring men meant I found myself in new sexual positions and acts, acts that I had gendered as feminine or masculine. I had associated being a top with being masculine, the one who does the penetrating. And being a bottom as feminine, the one who gets penetrated. These are phrases actively used by the queer community, but cis-het (short for cisgender and heterosexual) people can adapt this language too. Associating a bottom with being feminine and a top with being masculine is copy-and-pasting the ideology of penetrative sex between a cis man and woman. It's hard to escape the thoughts of heteronormativity!

Expanding my sexual pleasure

With my change in sexuality came a new realm of sexual pleasure. I started to have vaginal penetrative sex, even though I had always felt unable and equally terrified to explore this with cis women. That's not any fault of theirs, but because of the sexual scripts I had learned – as a man, I must do the penetrating! On one occasion, a long time ago, I was lying in bed with a girl I was dating when she pulled out a silver bullet vibrator. My immediate reaction was to run. Sadly, in executing this escape plan, I stumbled and just fell off the bed instead.

I didn't have the same challenges when it came to having sex with men. I found it a lot easier mentally as it didn't intrude on the notion of how sex 'should be'. And by that I mean the cis–het framework of sex, or 'penis-in-vagina' (PIV) sex. For that reason, I felt slightly more comfortable. Also, us both being men, and having the same expectations being placed on us, felt like it made for a more straightforward interaction. As strange as this may sound, having sex with men led me to being more comfortable in my body as I started to embrace the use of my not-so-wanted vagina., offering me an opportunity to connect with a part of me that I had avoided for so many years.

The one thing I didn't like about having sex with cis men is that they assumed that I would be a bottom by default. Although I'm happy to partake in some penetration, you can't assume that a trans man would enjoy this. Just as you can't assume a trans woman would want to penetrate someone. I cannot tell you how varied this preference is between any sexual partners.

I started to become more sexually confident. It helped that the more traditionally 'masculine' men I slept with stood firm in their masculinity. They didn't waiver depending on what sexual positions they played. Their confidence and way of thinking rubbed off on me.

Gender norms were fucking up my sex life

Much like in my general life, gender norms and expectations were fucking up my life in the bedroom. The anxiety that I felt surrounding this was killing my sex drive and robbing me of my ability to be present. Looking back, I can't believe I allowed that nonsense to get in the way of me enjoying good-good sex. The unfavourable magnetic pull of gender roles had infiltrated my sex life and I felt inclined to obey them. To resist and wander into unknown territory was going to require me to unpack beliefs that I wasn't ready to let go of. Because if I did, what would be left?

When I had sex with women, I felt like I had to be the top. Anything other than that would be crossing the invisible but very real line of heteronormativity. What I've realised is that gendering sexual acts does nothing for our intimate exploration. In fact, it creates unnecessary boundaries that limit both partners' sexual pleasure.

Penetrative sex with women

I was terrified of exploring the same type of sex with cis women. I felt like there were certain acts that I could only do with people of a certain gender. In other words, things that played into gender roles. Men could penetrate me, but I must penetrate women. So although it was something I wanted, a cis woman fucking me felt like a no-go.

This really affected my sexual and romantic relationships with cis women because I started to find sex with them less pleasurable as my sexual needs were not being met. I quickly realised I had put limits on my sexual interactions because of my own misconceptions. I felt like it would be in some way 'wrong' to allow a cis woman to strap me. Over everything, my biggest fear was being left emasculated. These self-imposed limits were stunting my potential for pleasure.

Being strapped by a woman

Then the universe came through for your boy and introduced me to a woman who I loved with my whole heart and, most importantly, trusted. I was highly attracted to her. Soft neck kisses would have me so wet I'd have to change my boxers. Fun fact, I was told that testosterone should scientifically dry you up, but it made me wetter than before I was on T.

I loved having sex with her. We had an incredible, explorative sex life. It was full of everything that makes intimacy exciting and safe; all kinds of positions. One morning in the kitchen, sometimes in public, next night in the bathtub kind of sex. And she was constantly trying to introduce me to a plethora of toys. We would always debrief after we tried something new. These post-coital conversations were a vital part of the process. We would ensure that both of us enjoyed the experience and we would ask each other how we could make it more pleasurable the next time. In the heat of the moment, nothing existed apart from her. She captured the attention of all my senses. I got lost in her. It felt like a spiritual experience. It was truly beautiful. After a few months of us dating, I asked her how she felt about trying to be a top and she was excited by the idea. So we got jiggy wit' it and gave it a try.

Bless her. She did an incredible job in attempting to confront my fears and reassuring me time after time that she actually enjoyed it and that it turned her on. It gave her a chance to explore more of her masculine side that she couldn't in her day-to-day life. She told me felt empowered by it. Although I struggled the first time, it got much easier the more we did it. I think what really helped was slowly introducing different toys and then building up to strapping.

Overcoming dysphoria

Dysphoria varies from person to person so I can't speak for everyone's experience. Over the years, I've tried many things to help quieten the thoughts that would eat away at me during sex. But no matter what tools I used, I always started with this logic: 'Well, if they didn't like me, they wouldn't be here.' Having a partner actually confirm that was the case would also be helpful. But even so, it's easy for destructive thoughts to creep into intimate moments.

I reminded myself that body hang-ups aren't something exclusively felt by trans people, although I recognise that a cis person's experience will be very different from mine. Even so, it was helpful to remember that a lot of people struggle with the way their body looks, so I wasn't alone.

Practising radical self-acceptance played a large part in my sex life becoming great. I had to accept that, in that moment, I didn't have the relationship I wanted with my body, but that's OK. It doesn't mean I'm less worthy of love and pleasure. But on the plus side, the growth of my mini penis (that isn't so mini these days) helped me to find pleasure in a way that validates my masculinity.

If you are lucky enough to find yourself in bed with a trans person, there are a few measures you can put in place to make the whole activity more fun and comfortable all around. Our starting point is always to not make assumptions about what body parts that person has and, to bring up my earlier point, how they like to use them.

When it comes to what body parts go where, that's a vital conversation to have with the person before having sex. In my experience, if my sexual partner understands my 'dos and don'ts' before we hit the sheets, it means they are far less likely to trigger me or do something that makes me feel uncomfortable. Treat that person like you care about them before anything else. To be honest, this should be happening between all sexual partners, not just the trans ones.

When it came to partners, it was important for me to choose the right people – those who were caring and understanding of the challenges I faced. I introduced boundaries and we both checked in on each other during sex to be sure we were both still present and enjoying it. A post-sex debrief gave both of us a chance to reflect on what we enjoyed and how we felt.

I would make sure I was checking in with myself too, and that I wasn't kidding myself about where I was at. I would assess individual moves and ask myself the difficult questions like: 'Do I like having sex completely naked – yes or no?' Let's say the answer was no. I would then ask myself if there was a piece of clothing that could help with that. For example, there are many trans men awaiting top surgery who would prefer to keep their top or binder on. I did for years.

Lighting is a big one too. 'The big light' may feel too exposing. If so, turn on the side lamp, phone torch or even get more romantic with a candle. When I was at the start of my transition, I preferred no light at all. It's going from maximum exposure to minimum.

Home in on those little details and the whole interaction will feel more enjoyable. If you're penetrating your trans partner (or any partner) with a strap-on, find out which strap-ons they do and don't like. It might be that they prefer coloured ones to the flesh-coloured variety. The size could have an impact too, maybe it's too big or too small. While you're talking about it, you can also take the opportunity to ask what parts of their body they like, then you can make them your focus.

To paraphrase the words of Miss Ariana Grande in her hit 'Positions', switchin' up positions for your partner is another huge part of enjoying sex, whether trans or not. Positions are a big one! Lean into those which feel the most comfortable. Spooning and playing with the little spoon and big spoon is a nice thing to do. Hit up Google for more inspo. You can change your height as this will add a power-play dynamic.

Language is up there with the most important elements of sex. You can ask if they have a name for their genitals and help them name them if not. My own is called my 'mini penis'. But others would call theirs 'T-dick' or cute names such as 'dicklet'. I personally use the combination of mini penis (which I used to refer to my clitoris) and vagina (vaginal passage). My favourite of all time for trans women has to be 'pussy stick'.

Then there are a few things that I never expected to help me connect to my genitals. On the men's weekend I attended run by Jordan Candlish, we did a potency meditation. It required us to breathe into our genitalia as it's a powerful energy source. I was shocked by how much connection I felt. I could feel pulses in my mini penis, as well as my blood circulating through. It was a wonderful experience. I felt so grounded in my body for the first time. I had never taken a moment to just sit and feel my genitals with no goal in mind, no agenda. In the past my genitals had been a part of my body that I washed, a source of sexual pleasure for others and for doctors to look and poke at. I had never really spent time feeling both my mini penis and vagina for me. It felt like I took ownership over my body for the first time. It was such a powerful moment that I'll never forget.

One of the keys to lessening dysphoria is definitely gender-affirming. A survey conducted by the *Washington Post* and KFF, a non-profit organisation focusing on health issues, is the largest non-governmental survey of transgender adults that used a random sample population. The questionnaire found that a majority of transgender adults are happier after transitioning.[5]

I've called this chapter 'Mini Penis!', and at this point you might be wondering why. You know I can't be referring to Rhino, a solid six-and-a-half inches of silicone manhood. No, a mini penis is an enlarged clitoris that is the result of taking testosterone. On average they are one or two inches long. Some people call it a T-dick, but I use the term mini penis and I'm happy with my choices. There are many effects of taking hormones in your transition, but for me, this is one of the best.

In one of my favourite books, *Queer Sex* (read it, it's so good),[6] Juno Roche, the author, gives an account of how she feels. She said: 'Transitioning has given me access to parts of my body that I never even had before. It's opened up possibilities.'

I feel the same. With the aid of testosterone, being able to grow my mini penis meant that while masturbating I could use more of a stroking up and down motion. Plus, when someone was going down on me, they used the familiar blow-job motion of moving their head in and out, which helped me imagine I had a full-sized penis. Being able to rub my mini penis against my sexual partners was a big turn on for me and in a way, that affirmed my gender.

Nowadays I find myself considering bottom surgery more than I ever have – because I want more pleasure in my life, and I believe vagina-preserving phalloplasty can get me there. Gaining a full-grown penis would bring me in closer connection with myself. I don't want to have one purely for sexual reasons, in fact I think my fondest moments will be when he – I'll have to find a new nickname since 'Rhino' is taken – is flaccid. The gentleness, the floppiness, the just existing.

These days, I find myself increasingly free of dysphoria. Don't get me wrong; in rare moments I'm sure it will rear its ugly head, but it's nowhere near being the main character in my life any more. All of the above has played an enormous part in that.

Once I had overcome feelings of dysphoria, I still had to unpack some of the restrictive beliefs I had built around sex. Just as I had to re-evaluate my relationship with gender identity, I also had to address the gender norms I had associated with various sex acts. Holding onto gender norms stunted my sexual expression. I wanted to have more mental freedom so it could unblock my physical freedom. I had to unpack how I felt about my body in sexual situations with different partners.

From my perspective, if you take the time to untangle a sex act from its 'associated gender', you would have a wonderful and explorative sex life. Separating the two means that you can try out new things without it negatively affecting how you feel about your identity. This is something many people in the queer community have already worked on, but I believe cis-het couples would highly benefit from it too.

I had interpreted movements to be masculine and feminine too. I didn't see masculine men move their bodies with Shakira Hips-Don't-Lie movements or be able to hit a quick twerk. A large part of what helped me work through this was watching dancers. I'd look at them and think: 'All I see is incredible dancers.' I didn't calculate how masculine or feminine they were based on how their body moved. But that's how our brains tend to work, right? We see others with a kinder lens than the one through which we view ourselves.

I know porn has a bad rep, but it helped me. Watching trans guys have sex gave me a newly found confidence. I watched them get fucked, do the fucking and sucking and all I could think was: 'Holy shit, this it hot!' That made me believe that someone else will look at me and think the same.

I put in the work and one day I just stopped caring. Getting to this place wasn't easy. But for me, I was tired of beating myself up and fighting myself. I was tired of being dictated to by how I should look and move. I was tired of feeling judged and self-conscious and as if my gender depended on my performance between the sheets. I started to fall in love with the way my body intertwined with different bodies. When I managed to release myself from that narrow thinking, I was free to try anything with my partners without it rocking my sense of self. Nowadays I'm living my best sex life, doing everything I want with any gender! It's liberating.

Afterwards I found myself asking positive questions like: how can I reduce the likelihood of my dysphoria flaring up when I have sex with a woman? How can I ensure that cis men don't assume I want to be a bottom? By accepting where I was at, I could take steps to make things better. I was no longer hiding from the truth, hoping that somehow things would magically improve. I confronted my discomfort and a more fulfilled life awaited me after taking that step. I'm a much more confident person now. Sexual energy is one of our most personal and strong forces. Once I had tapped into mine, I found myself taking it with me outside of the bedroom and into every room I stepped into.

Attraction

I think sometimes we skip ahead and forget to explore our understanding of the basics. When thinking through all of this, I realised I had never asked the question: how does attraction actually work?

I met Dr Karen Gurney at a Sex Talks event. It was a wonderful event that explored all things sex, hosted by the beautiful and intelligent Emma-Louise Boynton. After exchanging a few theories with Dr G, her enthusiasm and passion for this conversation left me thinking there is no one more perfect to explore this topic with. I posed my first, very basic question to her: 'How does attraction actually work?' She responded: 'I love that you asked that question, because the truth is, we don't actually know!' But don't worry, she didn't leave me hanging there. She filled in some of the gaps: 'We know that we will find different things attractive. We don't know why some of us find some things sexually attractive or visually attractive, other things not.' She explained that this forms the basis of our understanding of our own sexuality, and our sexual orientation.

As for why we have these feelings of attraction for some people and none for others, she explained that this is one of life's great mysteries, although we tend to group the people we are attracted to (often by gender) and then use terms like 'straight', 'gay', 'lesbian', 'bi' or 'pansexual' to indicate the direction of our attractions.

Something she said that really grabbed my attention was what we actually mean when we say we're attracted to men. How many of us have stopped to reflect on that? She asked if we meant their physical biology, facial hair, or do we literally mean their genitals? Which is something I've never examined in myself when it comes to being attracted to men, or anyone. Some people may say it's masculinity that they find alluring, but even so, this can be found in a number of places that they don't mean to include. Could that be people holding themselves in a way society classically associates with 'manliness', or anyone with a flatter chest? Dr Gurney said:

> When you break it down like that, a binary concept of gender — which many people subscribe to — it becomes a bit ridiculous. This is because masculinity is something that lots of people hold. Same with femininity. So, it's quite interesting, because you could relax those ideas of sexual orientation, just by thinking: *Well, what is it I'm attracted to? Could it be androgyny, that kind of borders on femininity?* And if so, that could be present in people of all genders.

This reminded me of a conversation I had with a straight cis girl friend of mine. She had only ever had sex with men, but every now and again she would meet a stud (a colloquial term often used for a masculine-presenting Black woman who is a lesbian) and become infatuated with her. She even once announced 'I would sleep with her' after a stud caught her eye. I told Dr Gurney the story and she agreed that it confirmed the premise of our conversation. She said:

> What your friend is saying is: 'I'm attracted to masculinity and, actually, the genitals that that

person has are irrelevant because what I'm attracted
to is the way they carry themselves.' In this instance
that could be the clothes they wear, the kind of social
positioning they take, or something about their
appearance, like the length of their hair.

As I heard Dr Gurney talk about these labels, I realised she was
speaking directly to something I had wrestled with my whole
life: defining my sexuality. In my teens I adopted the label of
'straight' and later moved on to self-identifying as bi. And now
I was understanding how wide the spectrum of sexual
orientation is.

I realised that I find people of all genders attractive – not
just men and women. The straw that broke the camel's back
was when I started to meet and desire non-binary people. They
are neither male nor female, so what do I actually find
attractive? Those individuals opened my eyes to see attraction
in a new way.

In light of this, I would say the term that best describes my
feelings is 'pansexual'. This is a word that's been around since
the early 1900s. It fell out of our vocabulary as Western ideology
of gender became more dominant. Much like the term 'asexual',
most people think of these labels as modern inventions but
really and truly they have just re-emerged.

It took time and deep reflection for me to understand the
unique make up of my sexuality; the body type I find attractive,
the balance of masculinity and femininity, the mix-match of
body parts. I don't want to close myself off from good sex or
good sexual partners because of rigid ideas and I'm pleased
I've managed to break out of those limits. But that left me
wondering, if we manage to update our mindset to agree that
sex and gender are not binary, do our categories for sexual
orientation even work any more? I'm not sure, but with our

new understanding of it, I, like Dr Gurney, believe we should loosen them.

If we were to evolve our language, what would that look like? On the dating app Feeld, which is designed for 'open-minded individuals', they have an orientation category called 'hetero-flex', which I really like. They explain this as: 'anyone who primarily defines their sexuality as straight, but has the potential to be attracted to someone of another gender'.[7] Dr Gurney agreed that, given there is no need to put gender in two separate boxes, it opens up the possibilities for sexual orientation. She explained that the classic designations are in place to identify if you are attracted to someone who is 'same as self' or 'opposite to self'. But this definition is left wanting when we accept that gender isn't binary.

Despite the fact that we can't pin down exactly why we're drawn to the object of our attractions, we can be more open-handed with *who* we find appealing. Dr Gurney suggested that many of us are crossing off whole groups without stopping to ask if there is attraction there after all.

Fifty shades of sexuality

Re-evaluating how we see sexuality doesn't come easy. It's natural to want to understand something within your framework. Boxes and categories can be helpful. They can create definitive lines that allow us to process things more easily but they're also very limiting.

I think the prospect of opening up the way we see sexuality is beautiful. We would have far more range in the people we end up being with and I believe dating people of different genders can be healing. So many women have learned through society to dress themselves and act in a way to appease the male gaze, but what happens when you find yourself with a woman? What happens if you don't feel the weight of that superficial pressure in love? What about the men who now feel comfortable dating other men? Perhaps that could help heal wounds around masculinity. Perhaps it can help us to re-evaluate what it is to 'be a man' anyway.

I'm hardly breaking new ground by suggesting that we rethink our narrow view of sexuality. It's a concept you've almost certainly heard about. It's called the Kinsey Scale. Let me introduce you to a tool that was instrumental in helping me get to grips with my sense of my own sexuality. According to Galupoa et al. in their research published in the *Journal of Bisexuality*, the Kinsey Scale 'constitutes one of the first attempts to acknowledge the diversity and fluidity of human sexual behaviour'.[8] They go on to explain that 'sexuality does not fall neatly into the very binary categories of exclusively heterosexual or exclusively homosexual'. The creators of the scale, Drs Alfred Kinsey, Wardell Pomeroy and Clyde Martin encapsulated the complexity of sexuality, and believed that sexuality is fluid and subject to change over time.

Those guys weren't the only ones to introduce a framework to help people understand the complexity of sexual orientation. There's also Fritz Klein, who developed the Klein Sexual Orientation Grid[9] – they do love to name these inventions after themselves, don't they?

This grid is way more detailed and informative than previous methods. It captures more nuance and complexity than the Kinsey Scale that works on a linear ranking from 0 (exclusively heterosexual) to 6 (exclusively homosexual). Instead, the grid focuses on seven different areas: sexual attraction, sexual behaviour, sexual fantasies, emotional preference, social preference, lifestyle and identity.

Seeing sexuality as a multi-layered metric based on many integrated factors helped me to see that it was beautiful and complex. For instance, I enjoyed being with women because I was in straight cis-passing relationships, so life was easy. When I was with men, I was more likely to be discriminated against. But the Klein scale accounts for this influence when it considers social preference. In addition, I tend to prefer long-term relationships with women as I've found them to be more nurturing and their love is more healing. That's not to say I can't find that in a man, but my experience has been that fewer of my emotional needs are met in relationships with men – possibly because men aren't taught how to be nurturing by our society. That's my emotional preference, another element that was considered by Klein.

'I just don't date trans people'

Rolling back to before you start having sex, the process of finding romantic partners is different for a trans person. 'I just don't date trans people' is a statement I've been on the receiving end of twice. In fairness, that's probably a lot less than most trans people.

The first time someone told me my transness discounted me from a relationship with them was when I was around eighteen years old. I had been speaking to a girl. She toyed with me a bit, talking to me about strong emotions and then withdrawing them without warning. She told me she liked me, but in the same breath told me she didn't want to take things any further. I liked her, so I ignored these signs and carried on giving her my time and attention. Like so many of us, I believed that if I gave her time she would come round to how she was feeling and put aside the whole trans thing. But she didn't and over the course of the summer our fling turned to dust. The final nail in the coffin was when she announced: 'I just don't date trans people.'

I'm not going to lie, I took it very personally. How could I not? I was never ashamed of being trans, but when you're in your teens it's easy to feel fragile about the things that make you different. I wanted to be loved for who I was, but who I was stopped me from receiving love.

I was older the second time someone told me they couldn't date me because I was trans. I was in my early twenties and I had developed a bit more resilience and emotional maturity. I was on the back seat of the 31 bus with my mum. We were heading home after spending the day in Camden Market when a cute girl sitting nearby caught my attention. She was with two friends and I overheard them saying they were heading to White City Westfield. The giant shopping centre had only opened two weeks before and it had been on my radar to go and check it out. This felt like the perfect opportunity to kill two birds with one stone. I leaned in to my mum and whispered: 'I wanna go where they're going.' She giggled at my motivation, amused that she had a typical boy chasing after girls. She whispered back 'Good luck, my boy' before handing me a bit of cash for the shops, then she kissed me on the forehead and jumped off the bus. It was a loving gesture but no man wants a kiss from his mum minutes before he's going to chirpse a girl.

It was a successful shopping trip, not because I bought anything but because the girl gave me her number. That kicked off years of friendship. We would talk on the phone for hours, she'd invite me to her family home, we drifted and rekindled, and she always made it clear how happy she was to hear from me. Even though we said it was friendship, I knew there were more feelings than that. Her smile was the biggest giveaway. It was obvious to me that she respected my identity; she had followed along with my journey for years. I'll never forget the look on her face when I hadn't seen her for a while and when we met up I had grown a beard.

It took me a couple of years to actually say out loud that I liked her. I told her on one of our long phone calls. She replied by listing all the things she loved about me as a person, but she didn't directly address my feelings. I felt like I knew what was coming next. Come on, we've all been here.

I pushed to get a straight answer from her and asked: 'You really don't see a future with me?' She stumbled on her words, really trying to find the best way to respond without upsetting me. In the end she said: 'I do, but I need you to have a penis.'

I burst into laughter, I couldn't help myself. Soon she was laughing too. That softened our conversation enough for her to feel comfortable to explain what she meant. She told me she found me physically attractive, but she didn't see us as sexually compatible. She just wasn't attracted to vaginas. We made a jokey promise that if I were to get a dick she wanted to be the first one to play with it. As devastated as I was at the time, I respected her for giving me that answer. Everything she said came from a loving place, but it just wasn't meant to be.

Our conversation was a really healthy one that was free of discrimination. She made it clear it wasn't because of who I was, it was because of the complexities of body, gender and attraction that we wouldn't work together. Had she just outright said the statement 'I don't date trans people', that would have been problematic. We all have preferences and things we do or don't find attractive, and that's fine. But ruling out a whole demographic is not. If you're willing to cancel out a whole group of people, it's usually because you hold a negative bias towards them. Often you don't believe that they are as worthy of love as others.

Plenty of people see it as the equivalent to 'You're not my type', but it's not the same. Genitalia preference is absolutely valid and I don't believe it to be transphobic. You don't have to date a trans person if you don't want to. Hell, you don't have to date anyone you don't want to. However, excluding all trans people from your 'who I find attractive' list is not right because what you are actually saying is you don't see trans men as men.

Lemme break it down.

Let's say you're a person who is attracted to men. You meet a trans man who is passing, has had 'all' of the surgeries and now his biological sex is pretty much in alignment with cis men, aside from sperm production. Would you date him? If you answered no, then why? Take a moment to think why you wouldn't date this man. Is it highly likely that you can only acknowledge the validity of someone's gender through the lens of the sex they were assigned at birth? This in turn would mean you don't see trans men as men – it is exclusionary.

The only reason that would exclude this from being the case is if you're AFAB (assigned female at birth) and you want to have a baby and you're completely set on doing it the old-fashioned way (no turkey baster for you). Then sure, that's more understandable. But if not, again, ask yourself why. Take a moment to think why you wouldn't date this man. I'm not here to tell you who you should or shouldn't date; I just want you to do some reflection on why you may exclude people.

Sex and sexuality can be an inherently personal topic and though no one can tell you what is 'right' for you and your body, I do think we can all take steps towards better self-awareness and more acceptance of others who may be or think differently from us.

7.

In the Media
While Trans

The first social-media platform I joined was MySpace. Tom was my first friend and all was good in the world. I had always liked the concept of online networking. Early on in my transition, socials felt like the only place I could escape my past and just be Kenny. Every now and then, I'd have a trans person message me for advice but that's as far as my activism went at that stage. For the most part I used social media as a way to connect with cute girls . . . and a place to post thirst-trap pictures. I didn't understand the power these platforms held back then, nor how important they would become in my life.

I joined Instagram in 2015, planning on using it in the same way I had any other social app. But Instagram was special. I found a feeling of community on there that left me wanting to share more about my life online. Using hashtags made it easier to find my people and it was so enticingly designed that I wanted to spend more and more of my time engrossed in its posts.

I found my timeline flooded with meaningful stories from strangers who didn't feel like strangers. Their strength became mine and, before I knew it, I was openly sharing that I was trans. Three years later and I found myself fronting the period campaign and falling into the world of activism. After that, not only was Instagram a place to express myself but it also became a way to create change. Don't get me wrong, I still posted the odd thirst trap – it can't all be serious on there.

On one particular day, I was suddenly feeling grateful for how at home I felt in my body. I felt like my physical form accurately represented my internal self. I posted a photo to celebrate the moment. It was a slightly raunchy picture. Me standing in front of my bedroom mirror, side on, showing off the tricep muscle I had worked so hard for, with a small–small flex. My hands were strategically positioned, covering my genital area.

I thought I looked great and I'd say by the comments from my followers, they agreed. But within a few hours the photo was taken down. I logged into my Instagram and saw the following message: 'Your photo has been removed because it breaches community guidelines for nudity or sexual activity.' I was pissed. The information they supply on their website to explain what this actually means is minimal. I believe that's intentional, therefore it's hard to counterargue their decision. So, although I had an account, they made it clear they held the keys.

I instantly appealed the decision. I'm not going to argue about whether or not the photo itself was inappropriate because that's beside the point, nor was it my reason for appealing. My point is, if it's inappropriate for me, it's inappropriate for all men. At the time this photo was taken down, and even today for that matter, you can find pictures that showcase far more nudity and sexual innuendo. Only these are from (mostly white) cis men and it seems to me that these largely go unchallenged by Instagram. For good measure, I did an experiment of my own. I reported a few photos of cis white men showcasing similar goods and I waited for the results. To my knowledge, not one single photo was taken down. Not one.

This is a familiar story if you're home to a marginalised group. I've seen this time and time again directed towards fat Black women. You may remember the campaign #IWantToSeeNyome, when plus-size Black British model Nyome Nicholas-Williams accused Instagram of racial bias after they removed a photo of her.[1] People were furious, explaining that social media was mirroring offline society in rejecting anyone who doesn't conform to Western beauty standards. One person said: 'Algorithms embody judgement traits of human moderators that feed artificial intelligence. Algorithms pick up on and reflect flawed human decisions as well as racial bias.'[2]

This bias also causes harm to the trans community – this is yet another way Blackness and transness are treated similarly. Just as with fat Black women, transness doesn't fit the priorities of the white and Western-centric world of the mainstream internet. Within trans masculinity this can be seen in the over-representation of skinny white transmascs (short for trans masculine, who are people that were AFAB but identify with masculinity). And the assumption of a particular image when non-binary and gender-diverse people are mentioned. I believe it is important that we don't see technology as neutral. Humans are programming the tech and their bias can be seen within it. In the modern world, with so much news and information coming from social media, we must be wary of what we take as truth.

When it comes to my picture, I'll never know whether the algorithm picked it up and hit the digital big red button or if a person reported it. That photo and its accompanying caption were a message of empowerment. It wasn't negative or political. It was just a good moment I wanted to share. The issue is, to some people, that my whole body is political.

The biases on Instagram and other social-media platforms are relevant and important because they demonstrate the ways that art and culture produced by the global majority is censored, removed, sanitised and criticised.

Language matters

So, when Instagram took down my photo, I decided to clap back. I appealed their decision and emailed a contact who worked for them, requesting he look into it. I suggested we jump on a call to figure this out. We spoke briefly and it seemed that a lot of the staff didn't know how the algorithm worked but he would follow up with the right department. After a small period of 'reviewing' my post, I received a notification telling me they were going to stand by their original decision. Annoyed by the outcome, I decided to post the whole thing on Instagram. Yep – the same banned photo, only this time with one minor change. I put the Instagram logo on top of my mini penis. I posted it along with a screenshot of the email I had sent. The caption said: 'Instagram removed my photo due to "nudity and sexual activity" so here's a version that may be better suited to their community guidelines.' A little ridiculous, I know, but you gotta have fun with your clap backs.

Tabloid paper and website the *Daily Mail* – or as I refer to them personally, the Daily Fail – wrote an article covering the dispute. The headline was: 'Transgender model blasts Instagram for removing a photo of him posing with his hands COVERING his genitals – saying men born biologically male "do it all the time" without censorship.'[3] When I read the piece my spidey senses tingled. I couldn't describe it, but something didn't sit right with me.

What bothered me was the language they chose to use. To me, it felt like they had gone for the most divisive phrasing possible. Nowhere in my comments had I used the term 'biologically male', but they did. The journalist could have said cis, so why didn't they? If this were an isolated incident, maybe I wouldn't think much of it. But, at least from my perspective, the *Daily Mail* appears to have a track record of careless headlines. Another headline read: 'Transgender model claims sanitary brands should be re-designed because using "pretty and pink" products targeted at women causes him psychological pain.'[4] That was about me too. And, unsurprisingly, that didn't sit right with me either.

It wasn't until I spoke to my good sis Kasey Robinson that I managed to make sense of why this was so wrong. With a degree in English Language and a Master's in Gender Studies, she was the perfect person to speak to. She helped me find the words to describe what I was experiencing. I felt like these headlines rang with 'dog-whistle politics'.

'A dog whistle' is the use of coded or suggestive language in political messaging that on the surface appears normal but has a secondary meaning that will only be understood by one group of people. The concept is named after ultrasonic dog whistles, which are audible to dogs but not humans. These 'dog whistles' use language that appears normal to the majority but communicates specific things to intended audiences.[5] They are generally used to convey messages on issues likely to provoke controversy without attracting negative attention. It's a very, very clever strategy and it works because the message hides in plain sight. It's almost as if we are wearing different glasses and you see one thing while I see another.

If we're taking the first *Daily Mail* article as an example, when you read it you may think, *well, OK, what they are saying are simply two facts, so it's all good*. But, in my opinion, that's how these headlines can disarm you and draw you in. The reality is, it subtly offers a comparison between me and other men – cis men – and I have an issue with that. In my experience as a trans man, when a person uses the term 'biological male' in conversation with me, they are doing so to invalidate my gender. It's a classic move that some people use to suggest that transness doesn't exist. When they say 'biologically male', they are differentiating between men, implying that cis men are more 'legitimate' than their trans counterparts. It's a way to discredit our identity.

These are microaggressions. They are subtle, negative digs at the trans community. They can be hard to call out and identify because transphobia has become so normalised in society. It's so commonplace, it's become invisible. For a trans person, though, they are much easier to spot. We know the things used to attack us – they hurt.

I'm angry about this because it directly impacts my community, but you should be mad too. There's a chance you're being played. These tactics are manipulative. Whether knowingly or not, many of them are trying to pull the wool over your eyes by using persuasive language around a topic you don't have experience of. When these tactics are at play, they are relying on the fact that you don't understand the lived experience of a trans person for this to work. It's something outside of your consciousness. To me, the media outlets that use these tactics are gaslighting the nation. That's why education is so important. We all need to learn to see through these tactics in order to help us stand against them.

We need to do all we can to stop hate in its tracks. If we don't, it will become increasingly visible, increasingly normalised and increasingly intense. When hate goes unchecked, transphobic attitudes can develop into discrimination and then to violence, and in extreme cases, genocide.

Charlie's documentary

Let's investigate another headline. My best friend, author and trans activist Charlie Craggs created a wonderful documentary highlighting the impact of long NHS waiting times on trans youth.[6] This is the headline the *Daily Mail* ran with: 'New BBC Three documentary "DIY Trans Teens" reveals how children can buy sex-change drugs'.[7]

Again, in my opinion, their language here is carefully chosen to incite as much outrage as possible. The first word I find particularly emotive is 'DIY' – OK, so it's three words but you get my drift. The use of DIY was actually down to the BBC documentary producers who named the show. I really believe they did Charlie and the trans community dirty with that one. What's the first thing that comes to mind when you think of DIY? It sounds careless and stupid. It belittles the gender-affirming treatment of young people.

Second, what do you imagine when someone says the word

'children'? Personally, I picture a little human between the ages of seven and ten. My mind would never envisage someone thirteen or older. I would assume that if that's the group you're referring to you'd say 'teen'. Using the word 'child' instead of 'teen' makes the people involved sound younger than they are. And with all the controversy surrounding trans youth, I think this was always going to have a negative impact.

When I asked Charlie her thoughts on the headline, she pointed out what a shame it was that it was portrayed as such a scandal. She said: 'We don't talk about people of the same age [as those in the documentary] being too young to make life-changing decisions such as joining the army, having a baby, smoking, drinking and gambling.'

Are you starting to get my point?

For me, the most unfortunate consequence is that we've lost a real opportunity to shine a light on the situations Charlie explores in the documentary. She covers valuable topics like why teens resort to buying hormones on the internet in the first place, the danger of long waiting times, or the fact that giving trans youth access to gender-affirming hormone treatment is known to reduce psychological distress by 22 per cent. We also know from research that trans adults who started gender-affirming hormone therapy as teens are often in a better position with their mental health than those who waited until they were adults.[8] These media outlets are making a mockery out of life-saving treatment.

I've seen the same emotive and charged language being used towards Black people, too. If you want an example, just google the different phrasing used to report on Kate Middleton and Meghan Markle.[9] This isn't just one newspaper. The crime is not solely with the *Daily Mail,* it's standard practice, particularly among tabloids. Another example is the *Daily Express*'s 2018 article that claimed to be worried that trans rights were 'hurting women and girls'. In laying out their point, they used words to describe trans activists like 'demented', 'madness', people who were 'bent on the subversion of humanity'.[10] They claimed that 'trans people were 'making a mockery of biological science', which we know is not the case, but to me it show a deep-seated bias towards what they perceive to be the 'natural order of things' when it comes to gender.

It's not just the language that people use in reporting but also the biased way they choose what to report on. Looking through the trans articles published in mainstream media, it's not hard to see that many of them are just looking to celebrate our downfall. When they have the opportunity to report on positive trans news, many of those media outlets are nowhere to be seen. For example, in July 2023 London Trans Pride organised a beautiful march with more than 25,000 attendees. The day was wholesome and encouraging, there was no violence. To the best of my knowledge, fewer than ten news outlets made any reference to it in their reporting that day.

Gender-inclusive language in the media

Another easy win for the media is to bemoan gender-inclusive language. 'It's the woke brigade' and 'You can't say anything these days' are standard responses to requests for more inclusivity. In June 2022, the NHS made some changes to the language they use on their website. In order to ensure they were inclusive of all their patients, they amended the pages that discussed womb, cervical and ovarian cancer and stripped back the use of the word 'woman'. The first sentences on the page about cervical cancer now say: 'Cervical cancer is a cancer that's found anywhere in the cervix. It mostly affects women under the age of 45. Anyone with a cervix can get cervical cancer.'[11]

Plenty of news outlets jumped on the opportunity to report on the NHS's new phrasing[12], but there was no announcement from the NHS themselves. I've wondered why they didn't make it clear publicly that they had made the decision to update the language. I think it could be for one of two reasons. Either they don't view this change in language as a big deal. For them, it may be a natural evolution of language and better phrasing that reflects society today. And/or they were afraid to draw attention to it, fearing a backlash.

It will come as no surprise to you that the NHS did get a lot of criticism for the update. It was all your typical suspects who spoke up. I think the right-leaning media outlets made a field trip of it. The majority of them were trying to push the agenda that the use of inclusive language would lead to the erasure of women. Judgements like these are rooted in the belief that trans people pose an existential threat to women. But why would we? Trans people do not want to erase gender. We know how important it is to feel seen, to be validated in your identity and to have language that accurately represents you. We want the same. We are all on the same team. We support the feminist movement, and we see trans rights as a sub-branch of feminism.

All of this potential harm to cis people isn't based on actual fact. There is far more evidence pointing to cis people being harmful to trans people, not the other way round. We are the ones who are discriminated against. I'm saddened that a perceived threat to cis women is prioritised over a very real threat to trans people.

I did a bit more digging and found a blog post by the NHS's senior content designer for NHS.UK written back in January 2020, which discussed making digital services more inclusive. The first lines read: 'It's important that we make digital services as inclusive as we can. People who can't access our services, who don't understand that a service is for them, or who don't feel respected and included, are less likely to get the health information, care and treatment they need.'[13] She also clarified that there's no universal standard for what makes language inclusive, so they consulted with a number of communities before settling on the right wording. I couldn't agree more: thinking through your language is a way to give trans people dignity while opening up access to healthcare.

I can imagine that the NHS would not have adopted the use of gender-inclusive language if they hadn't seen it as essential. It was a tool to help get more trans people to attend cervical screenings and that is vitally important. In a survey of 137 trans men and non-binary people with a cervix, only 58 per cent of those eligible had been screened.[14] Of the people in the UK in the population as a whole who were invited to a cervical screening in 2022–3, 74.2 per cent attended an appointment.[15] That difference is huge. Only half (53 per cent) of those eligible felt they had enough information about the screening process.[16]

There are so many barriers to cervical screening even before you add in a gender mix-match. Someone's culture, age or physically isolated location can all affect their attendance. Plus those who have suffered abuse are also less likely to be screened. Trans people can fall into these categories too, which just amplifies their marginalisation from good health care.

Part of the reason trans men aren't attending appointments is that many don't realise they have to. At the time of writing, trans men are not invited to have a cervical screening by the NHS. I know this because I wasn't invited. The NHS website states: 'If you're a trans man registered with a GP as male, you will not receive automatic invitations.' Whereas many trans women I know have been issued an invite.

I don't think many people stop and think about the real implications of not using gender-inclusive language and adapting systems to accommodate the trans community. It puts trans lives at risk. Cervical cancer is one of the most preventable cancers and cervical screening can catch it before it escalates. I had no idea about the tests until my sister Kizzy randomly asked me if I had been screened. Routine screening literally saves lives.

Petitioning the NHS to update their systems to make sure anyone with a cervix is invited for a screening, and anyone without one isn't, doesn't just benefit the trans community. Women who have had their womb removed because of cancer are still invited for cervical screenings. Imagine checking your mail and being reminded of that horrific event and what you lost in the process. With all the technology at our fingertips today, let's think bigger. Imagine the NHS created a slightly more complex system, while still being user friendly to their staff, that allowed them to input this kind of information and ensure everyone was cared for in a more personal and gentle way.

This isn't the only way the healthcare system fails trans people. I also have trouble using the online systems. In July 2022 I got a UTI. Annoyingly this isn't uncommon for me, I get them quite frequently. I wanted to avoid going to my GP for an appointment given how stretched our healthcare system is and how long it can take to even be seen. Instead, I opted to use an online doctor service.

I went through several different apps, but not one would prescribe the medication I needed. None of these services had trans men as an identity to choose from. When I followed the questionnaire through, I was rejected and told: 'We only prescribe cystitis treatment to women' and urinary tract infections in men [they should say cis men] should always be assessed by your GP.' I ended up spending the next six days without treatment, which left me in a lot of pain. Anyone who's had an UTI knows how uncomfortable they can be. I had to go back and forth with their customer service team to explain that I was trans and that I had a vagina. But I'd only receive one response per day, so it took a while to confirm all the details needed for them to dispense the medication. It was such a routine ailment to treat, and if I were a cis woman, I imagine that I would have been peeing comfortably thanks to my medication within a day. I can't imagine I'm the only one who's had this experience, and in my opinion, it's one negative experience too many!

There is evidence to suggest that gender-inclusive language is more beneficial to women than it is harmful. Studies show that it helps to reduce gender-based stereotypes.[16] It also may mean using gender-neutral terms which would serve to decentre men and level the playing field. Honestly, I believe this consistent concerned chatter about how trans people are going to erase women is more damaging to the health of women than the threat itself. The purpose of this more thoughtful approach to our words is making sure that everyone is taken care of. No one is taking away space from the other, we are expanding it. There is enough space for all of us. What the NHS did is commendable. We need more leading organisations to take a public stand on gender inclusivity. Because when one giant stands up, the rest tend to follow.

Mocking 'the woke brigade'

Sadly, not everyone shares my enthusiasm for gender-inclusive language. In the press, it's often the butt of the joke. Many see it as a sort of 'pandering'. I saw one headline that read: 'Now health professionals are urged to call vaginas "bonus holes" to avoid offending trans or non-binary patients.'[17] They aren't, by the way – this was another example of attention-grabbing headlines attempting to paint trans-inclusive language as 'ridiculous'. But health professionals adjusting the language they use to make their patient more comfortable is nothing new. Loads of women don't feel comfortable using the word 'vagina', but I've never seen an article mocking that. If using a different phrase allows a patient to be more comfortable, what is the issue? Plus, it has no impact on cis people.

Much of the media has a responsibility to capture the times, but we all know it can also set the tone as well. I hope this chapter has helped you question the subtleties in play behind selected headlines, and the potential risks that algorithms pose to perpetuating bias, so that we can all recognise and speak up as allies to effect positive change for trans people everywhere.

8.

We Have
to 'Protect'
the Kids

Trans youth are increasingly being thrust into the centre of the debate. Young people will always find it harder than adults to speak up for themselves and that's why they are an easy target. Also, they shouldn't be pushed to take a stand if they're not ready. Rightfully so, parents and carers would be reluctant to allow their younger ones to wade into the issue publicly, given how undignified these conversations can become. But this means the majority of voices we're hearing are those of adults, and a fair number of them have no personal connection with any young trans person. They don't have enough experience of what real life looks like for a trans young person, and all the research and stats in the world can't fill that gap.

It's no secret that we're living in a post-truth era. The tabloid that shouts the loudest wins and the most salacious headlines hoover up the precious clicks. And it seems there's no better clickbait than a bit of trans-related sensationalism. While there are laws in place to prevent outlets publishing false information and an Editors' Code of Practice that most mainstream newspapers have signed up to, there are loopholes. It's through these loopholes that we constantly see biased media push their own agenda. There are many headlines that tell you half the story and leave out vital context or variables. For example, we're all aware of the classic headline that does the rounds every couple of years. It's usually something like: 'TIME TO WINE! Drinking a glass of red is good for your health!' This will usually feature a brief and statistically weak study published in a little-known journal. It's news because it's eye-catching and feeds into a narrative that many want, not because these are the most scientifically robust, interesting or important findings that day. If you want a laugh, google the websites dedicated to listing all the thousands of things that the tabloids tell you will give you cancer. It makes for remarkable reading.

We need more responsible reporting (both across the board

and for trans-related stories), where journalists investigate, probe and review before just copy-and-pasting a press release. One of the factors that I think should always be taken into account before hitting publish on an article is: who benefits from this story? Who funded this research? And could either of those things make the findings biased?

Where there's a will, there's a way to twist the story to your own agenda. It's easy to find the results you want when you benefit from them. Then all you need to do is chuck a catchy pun in the title, send out a few press releases, book some influencers and host an event or two. Job done! Whatever you're pedalling – a product, service or even idea – you're well on your way to getting people's attention.

When I embarked on writing this book, I knew it was important to get out of my echo chamber. I knew I needed to truly understand the anti-trans perspective in order to directly address it. Friends told me not to read those opinions as it would only bring up traumas and pain. But how could I make a good counterargument if I didn't know what I was up against? It's not fun reading articles by people who disagree with your very existence. It was something I had to process with my therapist at times. But throughout, I stayed certain that I had made the decision that was best for me.

I've been an activist for a few years now and the anti-trans argument has evolved through several stages in that time. But not one of the new iterations has had any merit, in my opinion. First they said trans men were just women trying to escape the weight of the patriarchy. They hoped to discredit trans men and take the trans women down with us at the same time. Next, they insisted that trans kids weren't real, hoping that this would mean that by extension trans adults don't exist either. More recently, the stance dominating the headlines is that puberty blockers 'aren't safe'.

Puberty blockers

Puberty blockers are pills designed to hit pause on the physical effects of puberty. They were first prescribed in the 1980s to cis children who found themselves hitting puberty uncomfortably early. The medication was commonly prescribed for kids of around eight or nine years old, to hold off their development for a couple more years. The medicine was later approved by the Food and Drug Administration in 1993.

If you want the medical defintion, puberty blockers are in the group GnRHa (Gonadotrophin Releasing Hormone Agonists). Does that shed any light on them for you? No, me neither. But practically, they prevent the hormone signals that go from the brain to the ovaries and testicles that tell them to produce the hormones of puberty.[1] For those assigned male at birth, puberty blockers typically decrease the production of testosterone. This would slow the growth of facial and body hair, stop their voice from breaking, and limit the growth of their penis. For those assigned female at birth, they would typically decrease oestrogen production, which in turn would prevent breast development and stop menstruation. When a person stops taking the medication, their natural puberty will restart.[1]

The best thing about using puberty blockers is that it buys a young person more time. They'll get more time to really understand their emotions, so that they can unpick how they are feeling and work out if it's temporary or long term. It also means that they will have time to get their head around the impact that a decision like transitioning will have on the rest of their life. There's such concern in the media that a young person doesn't know their own mind and jumps to quick, irreversible decisions. Puberty blockers mean they can reflect and process without their body changing in ways that pile on the pressure and raise the stakes.

In 2022, the NHS started to restrict the prescription of these blockers without releasing a full explanation to the public. In what they say is an 'interim policy', they intend to limit its supply pending further research.[2,3] On their website, the NHS notes that puberty blockers are 'physically reversible' but that the physiological effects are currently unclear.[4] When questioned, the NHS responded:

> The NHS will only commission puberty-suppressing hormones as part of clinical research. This approach follows advice from Dr Hilary Cass's Independent Review highlighting the significant uncertainties surrounding the use of hormone treatments. We are now going out to targeted stakeholder testing on an interim clinical commissioning policy proposing that, outside of a research setting, puberty-suppressing hormones should not be routinely commissioned for children and adolescents who have gender incongruence/dysphoria.[5]

So there we have it.

There was no controversy around the use of these blockers until they started being prescribed to the trans community. I can't help but wonder if this decision is based less on the medical research – after all, puberty blockers are still being prescribed to cis children – and more on anti-trans groups hounding the NHS. If the medicine isn't safe for trans youth, it's not safe for cis kids either, right? The maths ain't mathing.

The NHS hasn't completely stopped prescribing the medication, but it's virtually impossible for a trans young person to get their hands on it unless they consent to taking part in a clinical trial. Even then, depending on the set-up of the trial, I assume they could be one of the participants given a placebo.

LGBTQI+ charity Stonewall said that it welcomed the publication of revised interim service specifications for trans youth, but criticised the policy surrounding puberty blockers. It said: 'This cannot be right. Treatment should be based on clinical need, and coerced participation in research is unethical.'[6] While Mermaids, the trans youth charity, reported: 'They [the NHS] will no longer routinely prescribe puberty blockers. Only those who are part of mandatory research will be eligible, which currently only includes those deemed to have "early-onset gender dysphoria".'[7]

When I read this, the first question I asked myself was: *what counts as 'early-onset gender dysphoria'?* It seems there hasn't been a clearly defined line when dysphoria stops being early onset and just becomes, well, regular onset. Mermaids addressed the question:'We also do not know! The diagnostic criteria is unclear, and the term is largely used by anti-gender groups.' It seems that most guidance uses the framework from either of the two main classifications of diseases used for diagnosis: ICD-11 (worldwide with the exception of the US) or DSM-5 (US only). But for the purposes of the gender-blocker conversation, these have been disregarded in favour of the ambiguous 'early-onset' criteria.

I understand that people want kids to wait before they transition. I get the concern. You don't want them to make big life choices at a young age. But this should be a decision left to that young person and their family. Have they stopped to consider the cost to a young trans person?

To me, the restriction of prescription puberty blockers was a devastating blow. The medication was life-saving when I was prescribed it at seventeen. I wish I had been given it earlier. My transition took a long time, partly because of the NHS waiting lists and partly because I was so young when I first went to the GP.

The doctors eventually gave me a puberty-blocker prescription because I had become suicidal. The intensity of my dysphoria built up over the years and it started to cast a shadow across all aspects of my life. I struggled to navigate the day-to-day. My thoughts were consumed by worries about my body continuing to develop in ways I couldn't bear. I felt so out of control. Puberty just served to reinforce the feeling that my body was mix-matched with my identity. When I started to develop boobs, I restricted my movement to minimise the chance someone would see them. I had loved playing football and I stopped as soon as my chest started growing because I didn't want to draw attention to it by running around. I would even slightly hunch my back, curving in my shoulders to make my whole front look flatter.

I had socially claimed my rightful gender, but my unwanted puberty caused so much pain in my life. It stole so much from me. I became ridiculously angry and nothing more than a troublesome teen. I stopped engaging in education, taking me from an A★ student to consistent Ds. I stopped looking in mirrors and eventually removed all of them from my house, aside from the one that lived in the bathroom. I never took photos of myself and avoided being in them with others. I only have a handful of pictures of me as a teen. I was so uncomfortable, I just wanted to hide. I didn't want people to see me because it wasn't the true me that they were seeing. I wasn't allowed to become who I knew I was, so instead I became a shell of myself.

For a young trans person going through an unwanted puberty, the cost is too high. Delaying treatment will only make them miserable. I hate the idea that other people will have to experience the same depths of depression I did before they are given medical help.

Diagnosing young people

The remarkable thing about children is how much more connected they are to their own intuition. As adults, we're easily swayed and can get lost in the steady influx of social norms that surround us. Kids don't ask themselves what's acceptable. They are just who they are. That's why I think it's important to listen to their feelings without denying or ignoring them. If a young person says they would like to transition, that should be taken seriously.

The next question that plagues debates and media coverage is: *what's the 'right' age?* Everyone wants to set an arbitrary age when we can definitively say that a young person is old enough to make the decision to transition. In my personal opinion, there isn't one. When is any one of us completely ready to make life-changing choices? You can ask any person who's quit their job or bought a house or got married and they'll tell you that big decisions come with doubts – it's natural. All we can do is arm ourselves with enough information to make a well-informed choice and trust our guts.

How do I know?

For those of you with a loved one considering what's right for them, I understand the desperate desire for certainty. My mum did a lot of research to help her understand how I was feeling and what my options were.

I'll be real, though: my journey to coming out as trans was one of pure guesswork. I started the thought process more than twenty years ago and consulted medical professionals a little while later. At the time there were hardly any trans people on TV and I knew none in real life. The examples I would see of transness in the media were people who were the butt of the joke and their identity was assumed to be nothing more than costume. The closest thing I had to a role model was Tracy Beaker.

LGBTQ+ rights group, Human Rights Campaign, explained the basics of understanding the trans experience for children and youth. They said: 'The general rule for determining whether a child is transgender or non-binary (rather than gender nonconforming or gender variant) is if the child is consistent, insistent and persistent about their transgender identity.' They continued to explain that just because your boy wants to wear a dress, or your girl wants to play football, does not mean they're transgender. Rather, it's when they tell you time and time again, over the course of months or years that they are another gender, that they are likely to be trans.[8]

Virtually everyone has a rough time around puberty. It's uncomfortable and we experience so many things at that time. We have these new hormones running through our bodies and suddenly all our feelings are big. We all ask ourselves questions about our identity. That's normal. But experiencing acute discomfort because your gender doesn't feel right is not normal.

I wouldn't change my experience for the world because it's made me the man I am today. But I sometimes wonder how different my experience would have been if my mum had been able to identify that I was trans and intervened earlier on. I wonder how much heartbreak and confusion it would have saved me.

As I said in the first chapter, there was an eight-year gap between my first GP appointment to discuss my transness and my first testosterone injection. Eight whole years. I had started working through my feelings when I realised I had them at three years old. I knew I was trans when I walked into that initial appointment. But as a young person I didn't have the right words to convince them to treat me sooner. I spent years being mentally prodded and poked while I desperately tried to come up with the most persuasive words.

I lost what could have been so many good years of my life because of the delay to my diagnoses. That's not to say all my problems would have been solved. They wouldn't. But being seen for who I was and allowing me to step into that person would have eased some of my pain. Shit, my mum probably would have let me socially transition sooner if she had had any reassurance from a doctor.

When a young person feels a mix-match between the sex they were assigned at birth and their gender, there is a four-stage care model. The first of those stages is assessment and exploration. The NHS explains that 'this means taking a holistic view of a young person's life. Like the relationship they have with their body, their medical history and sources of stress and the support they have in their life'.[9] Doctors use this process to discount any other health issue that could be contributing to how they're feeling. The young person would undergo a risk assessment for self-harm to ensure their safety.

At the second stage, they may start on some reversible interventions like puberty blockers. As I highlighted earlier, I think the time this buys a young person is vital. Next, in the third stage, they would be offered partially reversible interventions. These are gender-affirming hormones like oestrogen or testosterone. Before these prescriptions are issued, the person would have to have various tests to ensure the health of their organs, to make sure that they are suitable candidates for the medical intervention. Finally, they may decide to have irreversible interventions like a surgical procedure.

Young people need space

If you're concerned about a young person in your life who is exploring their gender identity, the best thing you can do for them is to give them space to work out who they are without pressure or judgement. In fact, that goes for a person of any age. They need a loving and consistent environment and people around them who allow them to work out who they truly are.

It makes an impact on anyone's mental health to know that they are accepted and valued, and so often trans people don't get that kind of warmth when they come out. The effect can be more far-reaching that just feeling disappointed or cut out. Studies suggest that trans people who are accepted by their families are likely to face less discrimination. They're also less likely to die by suicide, become homeless or contract HIV. I've been thinking about the impact of acceptance in my own life. Having my family, but particularly my mum, in my corner rooting for me at every opportunity definitely acted as a buffer to the nasty comments. Her 'no shit-talking my son' stance most definitely reduced how many discriminatory comments fell on my ears. And thankfully, since she was accepting of me, leaving home was never something I had to consider.

Some parents think that if they accept their child or give them space to explore their gender, they could make the 'wrong decision' and decide they are trans. But you can't convince someone they're something that they're not. If they're trans, no amount of persuasion from you will change that.

There's a famous case that illustrates my point. You may have heard of it. There isn't currently a Netflix documentary covering it, but no doubt there will be one in production. It's the story of twins David and Brian Reimer.[7] The boys were born in Winnipeg, Canada in 1965. They were healthy babies, but both had some trouble urinating. Doctors diagnosed them with phimosis, which is basically when your foreskin is too tight so it can't pull back. It's no biggie and can be fixed with a routine circumcision. Brian's operation went like clockwork, but sadly David's went horribly wrong, leaving him with a penis that was almost completely burned off. His parents were worried – and completely fuming, I imagine. Psychologist John Money told David's parents that he would never be able to have sex and, as a result, would not feel manly enough. He told them to completely remove his penis, surgically introduce a vagina and raise him as a girl. They renamed him Brenda and, on Dr Money's strong advice, never told him what had occurred. He had to take oestrogen at puberty and lived as a girl until he was fourteen years old. But it was around the age of nine or ten that he started telling his parents that he was male and even said he had a recurring dream that he was a boy. At fourteen, his parents told him what had happened all those years ago and by the time he was fifteen he had rejected his girl identity. Sadly, that wasn't the start of a free life for him. He underwent surgeries and testosterone injections to restore him to his real gender and suffered from depression. Tragically, at just thirty-eight years young, David died by suicide.

Dr Money was convinced that a child's gender could be dictated to them and that it was based on nurture, not nature. But this tragic story proves that isn't true. You can't convince someone to identify as a gender they aren't.

Tilly, Lucy and me

Gender is a spectrum and if you still don't believe me, go back and read Chapter 1 again. Go on, I'll wait here. How each person feels in relation to their position on that spectrum is entirely unique. I wanted to explore some contrasting experiences, so I've tracked the journey of three people who were assigned female at birth who all have different relationships with their gender.

Some of what's described will be familiar and relatable, while in some cases it will be completely new. But either way, it's valuable to hear about other people's experiences as well as deepening your understanding of your own. In fact, I believe it can help validate your own experience of gender. And maybe you can take our words as an opportunity to make sense of your own feelings or those of a loved one.

If you do share any of these feelings, that is not a trans or CIS diagnosis. This is not about defining those pathways. Everyone is individual. I think it's wonderful to explore a range of feelings that people can feel towards their gender.

Tilly is a thirty-one-year-old cis woman. She is an old friend from my school and my neighbour. To know her is to love her. There are few people with quite so much energy and honesty. You can rely on her to tell it like it is. I recently threw my tiny baby girl Cleo (my doggy) her first birthday party. I told Tilly other dogs would be attending and she, without asking, went out of her way to buy doggy cupcakes for them all. She's really there for her friends, that's just one of the many reasons I love her.

Lucy Spraggan is a beloved singer-songwriter who was a contestant on *The X Factor* in 2012 (the one James Arthur won). She was the first contestant in the show's history to bag a Top 40 single and album before the live shows aired – what an achievement. But to me she's just Spraggs! We met on a cruise (it's not just old people, thanks) and we instantly got along. She's a wonderful person with a bold spirit. And she boldly told me that when she was younger, she spent eight years living as a boy. At the time, they called themselves Max. The best way I can describe Lucy's story is that she is a cis woman who's had trans experience. Max wasn't a phase, she really was a boy when she was younger. I resonate with Lucy's story deeply. There are many parallels in the way we thought and felt.

I found it really difficult to choose my language when telling Lucy's story because it's a unique situation. When I'm speaking about the time Lucy spent identifying as Max, I will use the pronouns they/them. But when I'm speaking about Lucy at other times in her life, I will use she/her as that's how she identifies today.

A little pro tip from me: Lucy's situation is slightly different because she never transitioned, but when you are talking about a trans person's pre-transition you should still always refer to them with the name and pronouns they use today. For example, if you were talking about me pre-transition, you would say: 'I knew him before he transitioned' or you could replace 'him' with 'Kenny' – my current name.

The third person is me, Kenny, a trans man. But you know plenty about me by now, so I'll skip the introductions and just jump straight in – and even though you have heard some of my story already, I think it really helps expand our perspective on this topic to consider and reflect on these three experiences side by side.

1. How were you raised to see gender and the rules that applied to yours?

Like most children, Tilly took her cues on what it was to be a girl or boy from her parents. Her understanding of gender was based on how she saw her parents behave. She explained to me that her mum and dad didn't have set roles in the house – there weren't men's jobs and women's jobs. There were just jobs. The person who came home first was the one who did the cooking and childcare. As such, she didn't think much about her gender as a child. She didn't see rigid structures around boys and girls, so never questioned if she was one or the other.

Lucy told me a different story. Much like me, she didn't see herself as a girl. By the time Lucy was five years old, she had assumed the identity of a boy named Max. Everyone called them Max. Their mum was very supportive of them exploring their gender. Lucy reflected on that time and said: 'I was able to be whoever I wanted to be, because my mum recognised that you can't try and control someone's authenticity or identity. It doesn't work like that.' Lucy never 'came out' to her mum or had a discussion about it; she was just allowed to wear boxers and cut her hair short. She told me how grateful she felt that her mum allowed that kind of expression.

For me, by the time I could understand gender, I believed I

was a little boy. My mum did try and raise me in line with gender norms, buying me dresses and toys intended for girls. It was at around five years old that I started to reject anything I deemed girly, and she didn't force those things on me. Despite this, I did like the name Kelsey. It still feels like a part of me. But I didn't want a name that sounded so feminine to me, and in my teens changing my name was a way to mark my newly claimed gender.

Since we're talking about names, most trans people pick their new name and some stick to the one they were given at birth. My story was a little different. A close friend who I went to school with once turned to me and said: 'You're such a boy, I'm gonna give you a boy's name.' She decided she would call me Kenny. Some may have found that a bit weird or presumptuous, but it wasn't meant in that way. I found the sentiment endearing. It was heartwarming to feel seen at such a young age. If you're reading this, thank you, Jamelia.

Before I went to legally change my name by deed poll, I decided I would change my middle name too. At the time it was Cheryl. But that no longer felt like a good fit. My mum had always said if I had been assigned a boy at birth, she would have named me Ethan or Elliot. I didn't quite feel like an Elliot, it gave me drama-school vibes. But Ethan grew on me.

I knew adding the name Ethan would be the perfect way to honour her in the process. It was a gift I wanted to give her. I don't have children, but I can imagine that looking down on your newborn and picking a name that perfectly matches them must be like feeling the stars have aligned. That's how I felt when I filled out that form. This was a chance for a do-over.

I didn't tell mum before I did it. When I handed her the papers and she saw 'Ethan' there in black and white, she cried tears of joy. She said: 'I was going to call you that if . . . ' But before she could finish her sentence, I replied: 'I know, Mum, that's why I chose it.'

2. How did you feel about puberty?

Tilly spoke frankly about her experience with starting her
period: 'I feel the same way about it now as I did then – it's
painful! I have a different puberty experience from everybody
else. The first time I got my period, I literally passed out from
the pain.' That's a pain she still feels every month. But
interestingly, Tilly didn't speak negatively of menstruating but
rather saw it as an empowering reminder of her identity. She
told me that puberty was a 'springboard' to who she is now, and
her period is a monthly reminder of that.

When Lucy and I discussed the same topic, she told me that
she continued to live as Max until she got to eleven years old.
At that point puberty hit and she felt her body's changes forced
her out of her boy identity. She likened her developing to
unwanted ivy on the outside of a house – it quickly grows out
of control. She said she wasn'tt mortified by her period when
she started at thirteen, but even so, didn't see it as a gendered
thing. She said: 'I see it more as just what this vessel does.'

For me, puberty was extremely triggering. It felt like my
body was growing in completely the wrong direction. Before
puberty, my body felt neutral, it was a blank canvas that I could
dress as a boy. Once those hormones hit, I felt like I was
becoming a different person and I hated it. I remember my
breast tissue growing and my hips widening, and feeling like
my whole world was collapsing in. The world around me started
to affirm a gender I had no desire to be. I was attending an all-
girls' school, and surrounded by bras, periods and the word 'she'.
Throughout my childhood I experienced gender incongruence,
but at puberty I developed full-blown gender dysphoria.

3. How did you feel about femininity?

For Tilly, feelings of heightened femininity come and go. She
told me that there are days when she feels really connected

with it, and others when she doesn't. But regardless of the level to which she's conscious of it, she knows it's always there. Tilly said: 'I'm comfortable in myself and my femininity is just a result of my womanhood.'

But for Lucy that relationship wasn't straightforward. When I asked her how she felt about her femininity, she said: 'A bit lost in it.' Lucy told me about going to Claire's Accessories to get her ears pierced because it was 'such a fucking girly thing to do'. But measures like that and growing out her hair only made her feel like she hated herself. She explained why: 'Because I didn't step into being more feminine. I stepped into being Lucy again, which was a completely different person. I didn't know how to be a girl, I had lived as a boy. And I loved being a boy.'

I did give the whole 'being a girl' thing a shot before I left school. A few of the girls at my school were obsessed by the idea of giving me a makeover. I think they thought they were Michael Caine in *Miss Congeniality* or something. I thought it was ridiculous, but I agreed just to show everyone how much being a girl did not suit me. I didn't do it by halves: I wore the make-up, rolled up my school skirt and they requested and I even let them cut me a fringe – what was I thinking? I look back on those photos and think: 'Really?! Who were you trying to be?' My friends at school thought I looked cute, but everyone agreed that it didn't feel like me. The whole act of being a girl just did not suit me. For me it was just that, an act.

4. How do you feel about your body?

No one gets off without at least a couple of body hang-ups, no matter their gender. When I was talking to Tilly, it was clear she'd been on a journey with her body image. She told me that now that she was in her thirties, she was growing in loving her body and was in a healthy place. She said: 'Right now, I believe that I really do love my body. I embrace it because it's the only one I'm going to have. I take care of it, and I've stopped trying to compare it to other people's bodies. I think a lot of feminine-presenting people do that, but genuinely for me, I really love it. It's helped me go through some tough times.'

Those sentiments were in stark contrast to Lucy's response. She told me that she had never liked her body. She said: 'I've hated myself my whole life because I'm fat. So then I lost loads of weight and I was like: *Uh oh, I still fucking hate myself.*' She said that she started to realise those feelings could be associated with body dysmorphia. I posed the question, given her growing up being Max, that maybe it was actually gender dysphoria she was experiencing and she agreed.

After losing a lot of weight, Lucy decided to have a boob job in 2021. She told me that she didn't realise at the time, but actually that decision was a crossroads for her. She had also considered getting top surgery and embracing her Max identity. She decided to go ahead with the augmentation and lean into the body that she had. I assumed that she'd feel more womanly after the operation, but she didn't. Her choice of words really hit deep for me. She said: 'No, I didn't feel like it affirmed my gender, I'm saying it just reaffirmed the vessel [body] that I'm in.'

I knew I wanted top surgery from the second I realised it was an option. Although I loved them on others, boobies were not for me. Something about them really screamed 'girl' in my head. To me, they were the biggest thing holding me back from being a man. My relationship with my body got better when I started to step into my identity as a man. I really love my beard and the muscles I've been able to build with the help of testosterone. I've never been too bothered about having a vagina. But boobies, big no-no. I envisioned hot summer days topless roaming the parks of London. I could see myself posting thirst traps with a few too many buttons undone on a smart shirt. I could feel women digging their nails into my chest as we had sex. I was destined for some muscular peaks.

5. How you feel about your vagina?

If there is one thing I'm sure of, it's that Tilly loves her vagina. She told me . . . several times! 'My vagina and I are really good friends – we take care of each other . . . a lot!' She told me all this while trying not to crack up too much. But behind the laughs and jokes, it's clear there's a really healthy relationship there. Tilly told me that she decided to familiarise herself with her vulva at the age of seventeen after a friend challenged her to look between her legs with a mirror. She said: 'In doing that I've really gotten to know my pussy. I talk to her, get to know her and make sure she looks good. I don't do that for other people, just for me. But I check in on her weekly, that way I notice when something's happening or something's a bit off or I've eaten something different.'

Lucy, however, told me that she still sort of wished she had been born with a penis. When I asked her if she disliked her vagina, she replied: 'Yeah, it exists and it does its job.' But Max was furious they couldn't use the boy's toilets and pee standing up.

I can relate to Lucy, as I've said at times I feel like something is missing when I have sex with women. I didn't think much about my vagina, other than when my periods popped up. But a part of me does wish I had been born with a penis; maybe sex wouldn't feel like such a minefield. In saying that, I'm sure I'd just have different problems because life's like that. Hey, maybe one day I'll get a penis, but for today I'm good without one.

6. How often do you think about your gender?

For Tilly, thoughts of her gender are few and far between. She told me she didn't think about it much and didn't question her identity as a woman. In fact, the only time it takes front and centre in her mind is when she's with any friends who are trans as she's reminded of her privilege. She said: 'As a cis woman, I know I can use my voice for good to help the transgender community. Around trans friends I become hyper-aware of the privilege that I have being assigned female at birth and knowing I am female.'

Lucy said she frequently thought of her gender and that recently she had developed a new perspective on how to look at her experience. She told me that she had managed to work through a lot of the mix-matched feelings. As a result, she no longer hates that part of herself, as she loves Max. And that self-acceptance means that the world is her oyster. She said: 'If one day I wake up, and I'm like, *You know what? I think I want to be a man*, then I will fucking do that.' I love the way that Lucy defines her life through checkpoints. There are key moments when she recognised that she had a choice to make: to continue to be Lucy or become Max. Interestingly, though, Lucy did say that had she been given the option to stay as Max and if she'd been offered puberty blockers, she would have said yes to both.

When it comes to me, I've never second-guessed my choice to transition. Without a doubt, it was the right decision for me – all of the decisions were. Whether or not I do any more gender-affirming surgeries is the only question I ask myself. I recently started jaw filler, which is a non-permanent way of creating a more boxy jawline. It gives my face a fuller look which I think suits the way my body has developed.

7.   Have you experienced moments of gender euphoria?

When it comes to gender euphoria, Tilly's felt it. She told me that when she was younger she would have been considered a tomboy, climbing trees and playing football with the boys. Growing up, she did all kinds of sports: cheerleading, gymnastics, netball, rounders and rugby. She said: 'I felt gender euphoria every time I achieved something that people thought I couldn't as a girl. If I was playing rugby and the opposite team said that I shouldn't be playing and girls couldn't play, I would feel so aligned with myself and empowered by winning anyway.'

For Tilly, her gender euphoria is unleashed when she breaks beyond the boundaries that society puts on her as a woman. I think that's probably something only cis people feel. As she achieved typically 'manly' things like a successful rugby tackle, she felt her femininity and womanhood flourish, but that's something that can only happen when you're sure others won't question your gender. She said: 'I feel aligned with myself nearly every day. Even more when I do things that people say women shouldn't be able to do.'

Lucy had also felt gender euphoria, but when she was doing things typically associated with men. She told me she feels excited if she's ever misgendered and loved a drag experience she did a while ago. At times she's bound her chest and, paired with her impressive six-pack abs and a strategically placed cap, very much looks like an adult Max.

When it comes to me, without a shadow of a doubt my most gender-euphoric moment was the day I had top surgery. I had it done in Brighton, on the south coast of England. I wanted to do something to celebrate my 'no more boobies day'. My cousin Carla and I went onto the beachfront so I could bask in my glory. I threw my mum's makeshift binder into the sea and watched as it floated away. I've got a better understanding of pollution and the oceans now, so I can't say I would do that these days, but in that moment, all I could think was that I was so grateful that I never had to wear one of those again. The tears ran down my face.

Detransitioning

The primary fear for our trans kids is that they will change their mind. That they will grow up, realise it was 'just a phase' and regret the gender-affirming treatment they have undergone. It's a particular concern of parents and I understand.

Studies suggest that regret among people who have transitioned is relatively rare. In 2021, research pulled together the results from twenty-seven studies with almost 8,000 teens and adults who had transgender surgeries. They found that on average 1 per cent of people expressed regret. Of that group, some only felt this temporarily, while a small number decided to have detransitioning surgery.[10]

American researchers collected survey data from 28,000 trans people and found that 8 per cent took some kind of steps towards detransitioning. But of that group, almost two-thirds said they did so temporarily because of the pressure they felt, either financial, societal or from family. While the National Center for Transgender Equality asked why people were choosing to detransition and found that the most common responses were a lack of support at home, problems at work, harassment and discrimination.[11]

Of course, we have to acknowledge that detransition does happen. A lot of the fear around 'letting' someone medically transition is the worry that they will change their mind and want to undo those changes.

Understanding people who have chosen to detransition, and especially those who aren't happy with the way their life has gone, is vital. If we understand the processes that led them to both the transition and the detransition, we may be able to prevent it from happening in others.

When it comes to detransitioning, there are stages that are fully reversible and stages that aren't. Socialising as a new gender can be reversed and once a person stops taking puberty blockers, regular service is resumed. If they've been on gender-affirming hormones it can be difficult to fully detransition, especially for those who identify as trans masculine, because inheriting male features is harder to undo. It's slightly easier for trans women as testosterone is such a strong hormone. If that person has had surgery, things get more complicated. In this circumstance, the next steps would have to be taken on a case-by-case basis as everyone is different, but a lot of the surgical procedures would be difficult or impossible to undo.

A person who detransitions will also have to come back out to their friends and socialise as the gender they were assigned at birth again. I'm sure that this would raise some questions and lead to a few challenging conversations.

The reality of life, though, is that sometimes we get it wrong. Sometimes we change our minds. There are people who decide to have an abortion and may regret it down the line. There are people who get married and end up in messy divorces. Of course, I'm not saying these decisions are the same, because they're not. But they are big life choices that are likely to have a huge impact. It doesn't mean they shouldn't have been able to take that step in the first place.

Before we talk about blanket statements like 'protecting the kids', I do think that we need to do our research and get our facts right. This is a sensitive and weighty issue that warrants sensitive and weighty conversations.

9.

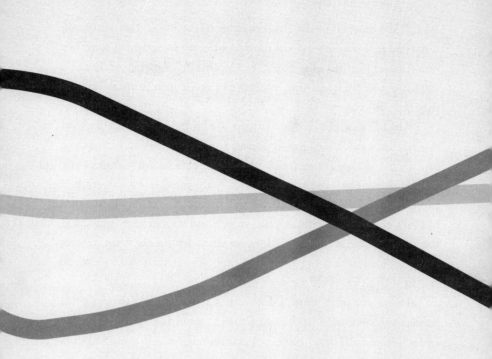

The Future
of Us

Woop! We made it to the final chapter of the book. I wrote it and you read it. We make a great team! But in all seriousness, whether you are exploring this topic for yourself, another or both, I applaud you for engaging with the content in a purposeful and meaningful way.

When I first came out as trans, I had no idea what was on the road ahead. I was just a young soul who knew I was a boy, but the world hadn't seen me that way yet. I had a vision of the person I wanted to become and with pure determination I pushed ahead, knowing that, for me, the only option was success. I didn't care what obstacles the world had to throw at me. I feel like it all makes sense now. None of those moments were in vain as they've provided me with the experiences that have allowed me to write this book for you.

Before we part ways, I'd like to say something to my trans brothers, sisters and siblings: I promise you, life gets better the older you get. All those concerns and feelings of self-consciousness will slip away. You will build more reference points to back up your belief that you are lovable just the way you are. When you stand strong in who you are, you'll find people who will love you and not try to change you. I assure you, over time, you'll curate a life that's worth living. It all feels like doom and gloom when you're in the thick of it. But all of the pain will help you to create a level of resilience that will enable you to achieve your wildest dreams. If the world is unkind and leaves you with scars, don't hate the world for the way it's treated you. Don't let your heart turn black because of those who don't have a heart of their own. Remember the words of the late Ruth Bader Ginsburg: 'It helps to be a little deaf.' Most people project their own insecurities onto others, but those are their wounds to heal, not yours. Learn to foster happiness in your life, despite the bad. Focus on the small joys. Don't get weighed down in the politics of your existence, you deserve to just be. Your existence will breathe love and light into the darkest of places and this will be your greatest power. Now get out there and show the world the power of being you.

To my cis sisters and brothers, as we spend our final moments together, I want us to think about one question: *what do we want the future to look like?* We should all be able to be ourselves, without fear of judgment. Personally, I want a world where everyone can feel free to be themselves. Where discrimination and abuse is minimal – or, better, non-existent. Where everyone is welcomed, feels loved and is acknowledged. Where everyone is safe.

In order to create that world, I believe, more than anything, we need to have a genuine curiosity towards one another. The more you learn about me and the more I learn about you, the more we can help one another. And that's what you've done here. Our freedom will be everyone's freedom. Advancing trans rights is at the heart of justice for people of all genders because it's all interconnected. Our movement aims to create equality for all.

So, what now? The real work of being an ally begins here. One of my favourite quotes is from Abu Bakr. He said: 'Without knowledge action is useless and knowledge without action is futile.' It's true: if you don't put this new form of knowledge to use, it's fruitless. While your understanding is fresh, this is the perfect time to take action. Now that you're equipped with facts, statistics and most importantly the right language, you're ready. You can do this by asking your workplace to take part in trans-related dates and donate money to charities and trans-related fundraisers, if you have the spare funds. You can also sign petitions, go on marches or have those difficult conversations with people who don't understand or agree with transness.

One of the questions I get a lot is: 'I have someone in my life who just doesn't get this stuff but I want to teach them – what's the best way?' I always recommend doing something that they love but doing it in a queer environment. Let's say, for example, your dad loves Formula 1. Take him to an F1 Pride event. I think it's always good to take them to their happy place as they'll be much more receptive. Or, of course, you can do it the old-fashioned way. Give them resources like this book or audio books or documentaries or theatre shows or dramatised series based on real life – you choose!

No matter how you do it, show up for trans people. Love and support them. Celebrate their milestones. When they hit one year on T (testosterone) or E (oestrogen), throw them a party! Get them a cake and decorate it. Buy them a gender-affirming congratulations card to go with it.

I believe my mum was my greatest ally. Not because she was perfect but because she stood up for me at every turn. She would always advocate on my behalf. She was my safe space when the world around me wasn't. And she showed me what love and respect looked like, to ensure I knew how to set the bar for others to treat me. She's no longer with us, but everything she's done for me will live in my heart and these pages for ever. This book is her legacy as much as mine.

Regardless of the type of person you were when you bought this book – an ally, a sceptic, or a loved one of a trans person – thank you for reading it in its entirety. I'm so grateful for you investing your time and energy into engaging with this body of work. I hope I've managed to answer some of your questions, address your concern and teach you something completely new. If you want to continue to connect with me, please do follow me on my social-media channels @KennyEthanJones. And if you ever want to talk, my DMs are open.

I guess this is goodbye for now. But I hope one day I get to meet you in person.

From my heart to yours,

Kenny :)

Further reading

Books by Trans and Non-binary Authors

Shon Faye, *The Transgender Issue: An Argument for Justice*
(Allen Lane, 2021)

Travis Alabanza, *None of the Above* (Canongate, 2022)

Schuyler Bailar, *He/She/They: How We Talk About Gender*
(Penguin Life, 2023)

Alok Vaid-Menon, *Beyond the Gender Binary*
(Pocket Change Collective, 2020)

Susan Stryker, *Transgender History: The Roots of Today's Revolution*
(Seal Studies, second edition, 2017)

Bibliography

Introduction

1. GLAAD Transgender Media Program. https://glaad.org/transgender/
2. 'Public attitudes towards trans people', Stonewall. https://www.stonewall.org.uk/sites/default/files/polling_on_trans_people.pdf
3. 'Transgender people over four times more likely than cisgender people to be victims of violent crime', Williams Institute, 2021.https://williamsinstitute.law.ucla.edu/press/ncvs-trans-press-release/
4. 'Transphobic hate crime reports have quadrupled over the past five years in the UK', BBC News, 2020. https://www.bbc.co.uk/news/av/uk-54486122
5. 'Transgender teens 7.6 times more likely to attempt suicide', Medical News Today, 2022. https://www.medicalnewstoday.com/articles/transgender-teens-7-6-times-more-likely-to-attempt-suicide#Increased-suicidal-ideation-and-attempts
6. 'Analysis shows startling levels of discrimination against Black transgender people', (National LGBTQ Task Force, 2011). https://www.thetaskforce.org/news/analysis-shows-startling-levels-of-discrimination-against-black-transgender-people/

1. Gender Begins Here

1. List of LGBTQ+ Terms, Stonewall. https://www.stonewall.org.uk/list-lgbtq-terms

2. Gender dysphoria, NHS. https://www.nhs.uk/conditions/gender-dysphoria/

3. 'Gender identity development in children', Healthychildren.org.https://www.healthychildren.org/English/ages-stages/gradeschool/Pages/Gender-Identity-and-Gender-Confusion-In-Children.aspx

4. Gender incongruence and transgender health in the ICD, WHO. https://www.who.int/standards/classifications/frequently-asked-questions/gender-incongruence-and-transgender-health-in-the-icd

5. 'Being transgender no longer classified as mental illness. Here's why', USA Today. https://eu.usatoday.com/story/news/2018/06/20/transgender-not-mental-illness-world-health-organization/717758002

6. Jürgensen, M. Klinische Evaluationsstudie im Netzwerk DSD/Intersexualität: Zentrale Ergebnisse, Slide 6, Presentation 27.05.2009 at Jenseits der zwei Geschlechter http://kastrationsspital.ch/public/Corpus-delicti_27-5-09.pdf and Netzwerk Intersexualität, Eva Kleinemeier, and Martina Jürgensen, Erste Ergebnisse der Klinischen Evaluationsstudie im Netzwerk Störungen der Geschlechtsentwicklung/ Intersexualität in Deutschland, Österreich und Schweiz Januar 2005 bis Dezember 2007, 2008.

7. '"I want to be like nature made me" Medically unncessary surgeries on intersex children in the US', Human Rights Watch, 2017. https://www.hrw.org/report/2017/07/25/i-want-be-nature-made-me/medically-unnecessary-surgeries-intersex-children-us

8. 'Fish are the sex-switching masters of the animal kingdom', BBC Earth. https://www.bbcearth.com/news/fish-are-the-sex-switching-masters-of-the-animal-kingdom

9. 'Five wild lionesses grow a man and start acting like males', *New Scientist*, 2016. https://www.newscientist.com/article/2106866-five-wild-lionesses-grow-a-mane-and-start-acting-like-males/

10. 'Seahorse fathers take reins in childbirth', *National Geographic*, 2002. https://www.nationalgeographic.com/pages/article/seahorse-fathers-take-reins-in-childbirth

11. Campos Barros, L.A., Rabeling, C., Teixeira, G.A., Mariano, C., Delabie, J.H.C., Cardsa de Aguiar, H.J.A. Decay of homologous chromosome pairs and discovery of males in the thelytokous fungus-growing ant *Mycocepurus smithii*. (2022). doi: 10.1038/s41598-022-08537-x.

12. 'Homosexuality: It's about survival – not sex', James O'Keefe, Tedx Talk, 2016. Available on YouTubehttps://www.youtube.com/watch?v=4Khn_z9FPmU

2. Black and Trans

1. 'A brief history of mixed-race identity', Mandem, 2018. https://mandemhood.com/a-brief-history-of-mixed-race-identity/

2. 'LGBT Issues in Jamaica', Human Rights First. https://humanrightsfirst.org/wp-content/uploads/2022/11/Jamaica-LGBT-Fact-Sheet.pdf.

3. 'The most homophobic place on Earth?', *Time* magazine, 2006.http://content.time.com/time/world/article/0,8599,1182991,00.html

4. 'Revealing a transgender transformation in Jamaica', BBC News, 2016. https://www.bbc.co.uk/news/av/world-latin-america-35459663

5. Arnold-Foster, Agnes. 'The queer Caribbean: conflicting uses of the colonial past', Notches, 2014. https://notchesblog.com/2014/05/29/the-queer-caribbean-conflicting-uses-of-the-colonial-past/

6. Injustice at Every Turn, Transequality.org. https://transequality.org/sites/default/files/docs/resources/ntds_black_respondents_2.pdf

7. Barnshaw, J. (2008). "Race". In Schaefer, Richard T. (ed.). *Encyclopedia of Race, Ethnicity, and Society. Vol. 1*. Sage Publications (2008)

8. Nova Reid, *The Good Ally* (HQ, 2021)

9. Sven Lindqvist, *Exterminate All The Brutes (Granta Books, 2002)*

10. 'The complicated legacy of Herbert Spencer, the man who coined "survival of the fittest"', *Smithsonian Magazine*, 2020. https://www.smithsonianmag.com/science-nature/herbert-spencer-survival-of-the-fittest-180974756/

11. Charles Darwin, *On the Origin of Species* (1859)

12. 'Natural Selection', *New Scientist*. https://www.newscientist.com/definition/natural-selection/

13. Neil MacMaster, *Racism in Europe, 1870-2000* (Red Grove Press, 2001).

14. Newman, C. 'Bartering from the BenchNew: A Tennessee judge prevents reproduction of social undesirables; historic analysis of involuntary sterilization of African American women'. *Georgetown Journal of Law and Modern Critical Race Perspectives* (2018).

15. 'Social Darwinism', History.com, 2018. https://www.history.com/topics/early-20th-century-us/social-darwinism

16. 'Accentuating the negative on race', Policy Exchange, 2017. https://policyexchange.org.uk/blogs/accentuating-the-negative-on-race/

17. 'Changes in DSM-5: Racism can cause PTSD similar to that of soldiers after war', *Medical Daily*, 2015. https://www.medicaldaily.com/changes-dsm-5-racism-can-cause-ptsd-similar-soldiers-after-war-246177

18. Cohen CI, Marino L. Racial and ethnic differences in the prevalence of psychotic symptoms in the general population. *Psychiatric Services*. (2013) 64:1103–9. 10.1176/appi.ps.201200348

19. Gazmararian J.A., James S.A., Lepkowski J.M. Depression in black and white women: the role of marriage and socioeconomic status. *Annals of Epidemiology*. 1995;5(6):455–463.

20. 'It's never too early to talk with children about race', YaleNews, 2020. https://news.yale.edu/2020/06/15/its-never-too-early-talk-children-about-race

21. 'Brown v. Board and "The doll test"', Legal Defense Fund. https://www.naacpldf.org/brown-vs-board/significance-doll-test/

22. '13 incredible facts about Stonewall legend and LGBT+ rights trailblazer Marsha P. Johnson you might not know', PinkNews, 2020. https://www.pinknews.co.uk/2020/08/24/marsha-p-johnson-stonewall-riots-death-institute-how-die-life

23. Riley C Snorton, *Black on Both Sides: A Racial History of Trans Identity (University Of Minnesota Press; 3rd ed., 5 Dec. 2017)*

24. 'Soujourner truth: Ain't I a woman?', National Park Service. https://www.nps.gov/articles/sojourner-truth.htm

25. Travis Alazbanza, *Burgerz (Methuen Drama, 2021)*

26. Edward Schiappa, *The Transgender Exigency: Defining Sex and Gender in the 21st Century* (Routledge, 2021)

27. 'No link between trans-inclusive policies and bathroom safety, study finds', NBC News, 2018. https://www.nbcnews.com/feature/nbc-out/no-link-between-trans-inclusive-policies-bathroom-safety-study-finds-n911106

28. 'Potential impacts of GRA reform for cisgender women: trans women's inclusion in women-only spaces and services', GovScot, 2019. https://www.gov.scot/binaries/content/documents/govscot/publications/foi-eir-release/2020/01/foi-202000011201/documents/foi-202000011201-document-5---earlier-version-of-literature-review/foi-202000011201-document-5---earlier-version-of-literature-review/govscot%3Adocument/FOI-202000011201%2BDocument%2B5%2B-%2BEarlier%2BVersion%2Bof%2BLiterature%2BReview.pdf

29. 'Home, the most dangerous place for women, with majority of female homicide victims worldwide killed by partners or family, UNODC study says', UN. https://www.unodc.org/unodc/en/press/releases/2018/November/home--the-most-dangerous-place-for-women--with-majority-of-female-homicide-victims-worldwide-killed-by-partners-or-family--unodc-study-says.html

30. 'Statistics show exactly how many times trans people have attacekd you in bathrooms', MIC, 2015. https://www.mic.com/articles/114066/statistics-show-exactly-how-many-times-trans-people-have-attacked-you-in-bathrooms

31. 'Gendered restrooms and minority stress: the public regulation of gender and its impact on transgender people's lives', The Williams Institute, 2013. https://williamsinstitute.law.ucla.edu/wp-content/uploads/Restrooms-Minority-Stress-Jun-2013.pdf

32. Tynslei Spence-Mitchel, 'Restroom restrictions: how race and sexuality have affected bathroom legislation'. In Verta Taylor, Leila Rupp and Nancy Whittier, *Feminist Frontiers* (McGraw-Hill Education, 2008)

33. 'Steve Barclay announces plans to stop trans women using female hospital wards,' *Independent*, 2023. https://www.independent.co.uk/news/uk/steve-barclay-nhs-health-secretary-nhs-providers-science-b2423017.html

34. 'Trans women may be banned from women's NHS wards', BBC News, 2023. https://www.bbc.co.uk/news/health-66994133

35. 'Women's single sex spaces in hospitals', TransLucent, 2022. https://translucent.org.uk/womens-single-sex-spaces-in-hospitals/

36. 'Colourism: how skin-tone bias affects racial equality at work,' World Economic Forum, 2020. https://www.weforum.org/agenda/2020/08/racial-equality-skin-tone-bias-colourism/

37. 'Human Skin Color Variation', Smithsonian National Museum of Natural History. https://humanorigins.si.edu/evidence/genetics/human-skin-color-variation

38. Barideaux, K., Crossby, A., Colorism and criminality: the effects of skin tone and crime type on judgements of guilt, *Applied Psychology in Criminal Justice,* 2021 16(2). https://dev.cjcenter.org/_files/apcj/16-2-3Barideaux.pdf

39. Ethnicity pay gaps: 2019, ONS. https://www.ons.gov.uk/employmentandlabourmarket/peopleinwork/earningsandworkinghours/articles/ethnicitypaygapsingreatbritain/2019

40. 'Dove apologises for ad showing black woman turning into white one', *Guardian*, 2017. https://www.theguardian.com/world/2017/oct/08/dove-apologises-for-ad-showing-black-woman-turning-into-white-one

41. 'Skin whitening: what is it, what are the risks and who profits?', CNN, 2022.
     https://edition.cnn.com/2022/01/25/world/as-equals-skin-whitening-global-
     market-explainer-intl-cmd/index.html.

42. 'Trans lives survey 2021: Enduring the UK's hostile environment', TransActual,
     2021. https://transactual.org.uk/trans-lives-21/

43. 'UK Black Pride is necessary celebration of Black queerness', UK Black Price,
     2019. https://www.ukblackpride.org.uk/blog/2019/3/8/uk-black-pride-is-a-
     necessary-celebration-of-black-queerness

44. 'Black history makers: UK Black Pride founer on creating change', Ham & High,
     2021. https://www.hamhigh.co.uk/news/21104300.black-history-makers-uk-black-
     pride-founder-creating-change/

3. Are You Going To Have THE Surgery?

1. Finney, N., Slomoff, R., Cervantes, B., Dunn, N., Strutner, S., Martinez, C., Vu, J.,
    Naidu, A., Hanami, D., and Billimek, J. Physical and Mental Changes Reported by
    Transgender and Non-Binary Users of Commercial and Non-Commercial Chest
    Binders: A Community-Informed Cross-Sectional Observational Study, Transgender
    Health (2023). doi: 10.1089/trgh.2023.0051

2. Gender Identity Clinic, UK. https://gic.nhs.uk/appointments/waiting-times/

3. Henderson, N., Selwyn, V., Beezhold, J., Howard, R., Gilmore, R., Bartolome, I. The
    impact of Gender Identity Clinic waiting times on the mental health of transitioning
    individuals, Eur Psychiatry (2022). doi: 10.1192/j.eurpsy.2022.2205

4. Gender Construction Kit. https://genderkit.org.uk/article/phalloplasty/

5. Gender Construction Kit. https://genderkit.org.uk/article/vaginoplasty/

4. My Legacy: The First Trans Man to Front a Period Campaign

1. 'I'm a short, transgender man who modelled at London Fashion Week to show that
    fashion can be diverse', Metro, 2019. https://metro.co.uk/2019/03/10/im-a-short-
    transgender-man-who-modelled-at-london-fashion-week-to-show-that-fashion-
    can-be-diverse-8796525/

2. The Menstrual Revolution booklet. FEWE, 2022.

3. Weekley, E. 'An etymological dictionary of modern English'. Courier Corporation (2012).

4. 'Why and when did menstruation become taboo?', Your Period Called, 2021. https://
    yourperiodcalled.com/2021/01/13/how-did-menstruation-become-a-taboo/

5. Sara Pascoe, Animal (Faber and Faber, 2016)

6. 'Why and when did menstruation become taboo?', Your Period Called, 2021. https://
    yourperiodcalled.com/2021/01/13/how-did-menstruation-become-a-taboo/

7. 'A history of menstruation: 5 interesting facts', TOTM, 2021. https://www.totm.
    com/history-menstruation-5-interesting-facts/

8. 'How did menstruation become taboo?', Clue, 2021. https://helloclue.com/articles/
    culture/how-did-menstruation-become-taboo

9. Why and when did menstruation become taboo?' Your Period Called, 2021. https://
    yourperiodcalled.com/2021/01/13/how-did-menstruation-become-a-taboo/

10.   'Chhaupadi and menstruation taboos', Action Aid. https://www.actionaid.org.uk/our-work/period-poverty/chhaupadi-and-menstruation-taboos

11.   Bloody Good Period charity. www.bloodygoodperiod.com

12.   'What did people use before pads and tampons?', Voxapod, 2021. https://voxapod.com/blogs/journal/the-history-of-menstrual-products

13.   'Mary Kenner (1912–2006), Blackpast.org, 2020. https://www.blackpast.org/african-american-history/mary-kenner-1912-2006/

14.   'This is the actual reason pad commercials use that weird blue liquid', Bustle, 2017. https://www.bustle.com/p/why-do-period-product-commercials-use-blue-liquid-the-practice-has-a-long-bizarre-history-2957963

15.   Klara Rydstrom, 'Degendering menstruation: making trans menstruators matter'. In Chris Bobel, Inga T. Winkler, Breanne Fahs, Katie Ann Hasson, Elizabeth Arveda Kissling, Tomi-Ann Roberts, *The Palgrave Handbook of Critical Menstruation Studies* (Palgrave Macmillan, 2020)

16.   Chrisler, J.C., Gorman, J.A., Manion, J., Murgo, M., Barney, A., Adams-Clark, A., Newton, J.R., McGrath, M. Queer periods: attitudes toward and experiences with menstruation in the masculine of centre and transgender community. *Cult Health Sex* (2016). doi: 10.1080/13691058.2016.1182645

17.   'Almost half of girls aged 14–21 are embarrassed by their periods', PLAN International, 2017. https://plan-uk.org/media-centre/almost-half-of-girls-aged-14-21-are-embarrassed-by-their-periods

18.   J.K. Rowling, X (formerly Twitter). https://twitter.com/jk_rowling/status/1269382518362509313

19.   'Asda praised for changing the name of "feminine hygiene" aisle', Yahoo! Life, 2022. www.uk.style.yahoo.com/asda-feminine-hygiene-aisle-period-tampon-pad-195404766.html

20.   'Boots renames "feminine hygiene" aisle to "period products"', *Independent*, 2022. https://www.independent.co.uk/life-style/boots-period-products-inclusive-b2053631.html

21.   Lost Fame periodcare brand. www.lostfame.com

5. Masculinity and Me

1.   'The Meaning of Masculinities', National Democratic Institute. https://www.ndi.org/sites/default/files/ACFrOgAZ9X_S2Bl-K9iPv3XhiQ140Fw6QWeUNSQwJwuNXzShO1b_Wv9-Vbsw1KX0rkmdxRZ-nlwzPhL-WIQLh1agPgzn5s70jFg-wYO0cIafAvyfqfNvFQQX_UYSZKGjzuPLlyl2J_UFqRjaCxNs.pdf

2.   'On gender differences, no consensus on nature vs. nurture', Pew Research Centre, 2017. https://www.pewresearch.org/social-trends/2017/12/05/on-gender-differences-no-consensus-on-nature-vs-nurture/

3.   'From 4000 BCE to today: the fascinating history of men and makeup', Byrdie, 2020. https://www.byrdie.com/history-makeup-gender

4.   'Why did men stop wearing high heels', BBC News, 2013. https://www.bbc.co.uk/news/magazine-21151350

5.   'On gender differences, no consensus on nature vs. nurture', Pew Research Centre, 2017. https://www.pewresearch.org/social-trends/2017/12/05/on-gender-differences-no-consensus-on-nature-vs-nurture/

6. *Ibid.*

7. Hypermasculinity definition from EIGE. https://eige.europa.eu/publications-resources/thesaurus/terms/1381?language_content_entity

8. 'What is toxic masculinity', Very Well Mind, 2022. https://www.verywellmind.com/what-is-toxic-masculinity-5075107

9. Toxic masculinity vs. healthy masculinity, Green Hill Recovery. https://greenhillrecovery.com/toxic-masculinity-vs-healthy-masculinity/

10. 'Breaking the mould: navigating toxic masculinity in relationship,' Hope Therapy and Counselling Services, 2023. https://www.counselling-directory.org.uk/memberarticles/breaking-the-mould-navigating-toxic-masculinity-in-relationship

11. 'The dangerous effects of toxic masculinity', Very Well Mind, 2023. https://www.verywellmind.com/the-dangerous-mental-health-effects-of-toxic-masculinity-5073957

12. Dr Julie Smith, *Why Has Nobody Told Me This Before* (Michael Joseph, 2022)

13. Dr Nicola LePera, *How to Do the Work* (Orion Spring, 2021)

14. Emotional Literacy definition from Twinkl. https://www.twinkl.co.uk/teaching-wiki/emotional-literacy

15. 'The feelings wheel: unlock the power of your emotions', Calm, 2023. https://www.calm.com/blog/the-feelings-wheel

16. 'What is distress tolerance?', Very Well Mind, 2020. https://www.verywellmind.com/distress-tolerance-2797294

17. https://www.jordancandlish.com/

18. 'Men urged to talk about mental healthy to prevent suicide', GOV.UK, 2022. www.gov.uk/government/news/men-urged-to-talk-about-mental-health-to-prevent-suicide

6. Mini Penis!

1. Colton Meier, S., Pardo, S.T., Labuski, C., Babcock, J. Measures of Clinical Health among Female-to-Male Transgender Person as a Funciton of Sexual Orientation. *Archives of Sexual Behaviour*, 2013. doi: 10.1007/s10508-012-0052-2

2. Lawrence, A.A. Sexuality Before and After Male-to-Female Sex Reassignment Surgery. Archives of Sexual Behaviour, 2004. doi: 10.1007/s10508-005-1793-y

3. UN Free & Equal definitions. https://www.unfe.org/definitions/

4. *Ibid.*

5. 'Majority of trans adults are happier after transitioning, survey finds', *Guardian*, 2023. https://www.theguardian.com/society/2023/mar/24/majority-trans-adults-happier-transitioning-survey

6. Juno Roche, *Queer Sex* (Jessica Kingsley Publishers, 2018)

7. 'Heteroflexible meaning: definition, history, and lifestyle', Feeld, 2023. https://feeld.co/blog/feeld-guides/what-is-heteroflexibility

8. Paz Galupo, M. Sexual Minority Reflections on the Kinsey Scale and the Klein Sexual Orientation Grid: Conceptualization and Measurement. Journal of Bisexuality, 2014. doi: 10.1080/15299716.2014.929553

9. Klein Sexual Orientation Grid, Bi.org. https://bi.org/en/klein-grid

7. In the Media While Trans

1. 'What's the story behind #IWantToSeeNyome? Medium, 2020. https://annechawrites.medium.com/whats-the-story-behind-iwanttoseenyome-7e9255f22452

2. 'The algorithms that detect hate speech online are biased against black people', Vox, 2019. https://www.vox.com/recode/2019/8/15/20806384/social-media-hate-speech-bias-black-african-american-facebook-twitter

3. 'Transgender model blasts Instagram for removing a photo of him posing with his hands covering his genitals – saying men born biologically male 'do it all the time" without censorship', *Daily Mail*, 2019. https://www.dailymail.co.uk/femail/article-7680619/Trans-man-rages-Instagram-removes-photo-hand-genitals.html

4. 'Transgender model claims sanitary brands should be re-designed because using "pretty and pink" products targeted at women causes him psychological pain", *Daily Mail*, 2020. https://www.dailymail.co.uk/femail/article-7886421/Transgender-model-claims-using-pretty-pink-sanitary-products-causes-psychological-pain.html

5. 'Dog Whistles', Social Workers Union blog series, 2023. https://swu-union.org.uk/wp-content/uploads/SWU-blog-series-Dog-Whistles-2023.pdf

6. Transitioning Teens, BBC Three. First broadcast August 2021. www.bbc.co.uk/programmes/p093wyx7

7. 'New BBC Three documentary "DIY Trans Teens" reveals how children can buy sex-change drugs', *Daily Mail*, 2021. https://www.dailymail.co.uk/news/article-9180377/New-BBC-Three-documentary-DIY-Trans-Teens-reveals-children-buy-sex-change-drugs.html

8. 'Better mental health found among transgender people who started hormones as teens', *Stanford Medicine*, 2022 https://med.stanford.edu/news/all-news/2022/01/mental-health-hormone-treatment-transgender-people.html

9. 'Fans call out "double standard" as Kate Middleton sports updo after Meghan Markle's bun "broke protocol"', *Independent*, 2023. https://www.independent.co.uk/life-style/royal-family/meghan-markle-kate-middleton-bun-protocol-b2420731.html

10. 'We must halt this transgender madness – it is hurting women and girls, blasts Leo McKinstry', *Daily Express*, 2020. https://www.express.co.uk/comment/columnists/leo-mckinstry/903140/Transgenderism-harming-women-must-be-stopped

11. Cervical cancer, NHS. https://www.nhs.uk/conditions/cervical-cancer/

12. 'Inclusive, gender-neutral language helps us all – it doesn't take away "woman-ness"', *Independent*, 2022. https://www.independent.co.uk/voices/inclusive-language-gender-neutral-trans-nhs-b2098314.html

13. Making digital services more inclusive, NHS. https://digital.nhs.uk/blog/transformation-blog/2020/making-digital-services-more-inclusive

14. Berner, A.M., Connolly, D.J., Pinnell, I., Wolton, A., MacNaughton, A., Challen, C., Nambiar, K., Bayliss, J., Barratt, J., Richards, C., Attitudes of transgender men and non-binary people to cervical screeing: a cross-sectional mixed-methods study in the UK. Br J Gen Pract, 2021. doi: 10.3399/BJGP.2020.0905

15. Cervical Screening Programmme, England – 2022–2023, NHS. https://digital.nhs.uk/data-and-information/publications/statistical/cervical-screening-annual/england-2022-2023

16. Berner, A.M., Connolly, D.J., Pinnell, I., Wolton, A., MacNaughton, A., Challen, C., Nambiar, K., Bayliss, J., Barratt, J., Richards, C., Attitudes of transgender men and non-binary people to cervical screeing: a cross-sectional mixed-methods study in the UK. Br J Gen Pract, 2021. doi: 10.3399/BJGP.2020.0905

17. 'How to use gender-neutral language, and why it's important to try', *Forbes*, 2020. https://www.forbes.com/sites/kimelsesser/2020/07/08/how-to-use-gender-neutral-language-and-why-its-important-to-try/

18. 'Now health professionals are urged to call vaginas "bonus holes" to avoid oddending trans or non-binary patient', *Daily Mail*, 2023. https://www.dailymail.co.uk/news/article-12274419/Now-health-professionals-urged-call-vaginas-bonus-holes-avoid-offending-patients.html

8. We Have to 'Protect' the Kids

1. 'Are puberty blockers reversible?', GenderGP.com, 2020. https://www.gendergp.com/are-puberty-blockers-reversible/

2. 'Are puberty blockers permanent? What you should know before treatment', Healthline. https://www.healthline.com/health/are-puberty-blockers-reversible

3. 'NHS England is trying to further limit trans youth's healthcare: here's how you can take action', Mermaids UK, 2023. https://mermaidsuk.org.uk/news/category/healthcare/

4. 'Interim Clinical Policy: puberty supressing hormones for children and adolescents who have gender incongruence/dysphoria', NHS England, 2023. https://www.engage.england.nhs.uk/consultation/puberty-suppressing-hormones/

5. 'Worried about your gender identity? Advice for teenagers', NHS. https://www.nhs.uk/live-well/trans-teenager

6. 'Implementing advice from the Cass Review', NHS England, 2023. https://www.england.nhs.uk/commissioning/spec-services/npc-crg/gender-dysphoria-clinical-programme/implementing-advice-from-the-cass-review/

7. 'Stonewall statement on NHS England's final Interim Service Specification for youth gender services', Stonewall, 2023. https://www.stonewall.org.uk/about-us/news/stonewall-statement-nhs-englands-final-interim-service-specification-youth-gender

8. 'New NHS England guidelines restricting future access to puberty blockers', Mermaids UK, 2023. https://mermaidsuk.org.uk/news/new-nhs-england-guidelines-restricting-future-access-to-puberty-blockers-our-analysis

9. 'Transgender children and youth: understanding the basics', Human Rights Campaign. https://www.gendergp.com/are-puberty-blockers-reversible/

10. GIDS, https://gids.nhs.uk/young-people/puberty-and-physical-intervention/

11. Bustos, V.P., Bustos, S.S., Mascaro, A., Del Corral, G., Forte, A.J., Ciudad, P., Kim, E.A., Langstein, H.N., Manrique, O.J. Regret after Gender-affirmation Surgery: A Systematic Review and Meta-analysis of Prevalence. *Plast Reconstr Surg Glob Open* (2021). doi: 10.1097/GOX.0000000000003477

12. Turban, J.L., Loo, S.S., Almazan, A.N., Keuroghlian, A.S. Factors Leading to 'Detransition' Among Transgender and Gender Diverse People in the United States: A Mixed-Methods Analysis. *LGBT Health* (2021). doi: 10.1089/lgbt.2020.0437

Acknowledgements

I've always loved the concept of books. They are incredible. You have the privilege of writing a body of work that lives beyond you and can impact thousands, if not millions, of people. As a man who cares about his legacy and wants to influence change on a large scale, they speak to me deeply.

I first had the idea for this book in 2019 and although I believe I can do anything I set my mind to, I wasn't sure if I was ready to write a book.

Writing a book, although it's a solo adventure, is a team effort to get it across the finishing line. There are many people I want to thank for helping get this book into your hands.

My literary agent, Lauren Gardener, came into my life shortly after the thought of wanting to write a book. She slid into my emails with confidence and praise! She had followed my journey on Instagram and wholeheartedly believed people needed to read my story. I signed with her and I couldn't have made a better decision. She's such a loving and nurturing woman. She's reassured me, advocated for me (get paid your worth!) and held my hand throughout this whole wild book-writing process.

Cheers to the first of many for us, Twinise next!

Marleigh Price, my original editor. Conversations with her felt like being two peas in a pod. She really saw my vision and believed in what I wanted to achieve with this book. Her passion for equality and her big heart made her my perfect match. She didn't stay along for the journey of finishing this book as she got offered a job she couldn't turn down. But her belief in this book at such an early stage only increased my motivation and caused me to have a bigger vision for this project.

Then came along Izzy Holton and Elizabeth Neep. By this point I had made good progress but I started to feel overwhelmed with the amount of work still left to do. Izzy's emotional intelligence is her superpower and her reassurance in my work gave me the strength to push through. Elizabeth is a very clever woman, always coming up with fantastic ideas and constantly smiling on our video calls (I really loved that). Their skill sets complemented each other, and with me in the middle, we made the perfect team! I'm so grateful I got to create my first book with them.

My co-writer, Lauren Windle. Let me tell you something about Lauren! She's witty, really good at what she does and fun to work with. Having her join the team felt like a massive weight being lifted off my shoulders. She took this book from being a really good body of work to a beautiful memoir and manifesto that wholeheartedly feels like an extension of everything that I am. She found words for me when I struggled to describe what I meant. She keeps us on track for the deadline and she really brought out the best in my writing. I'll be forever grateful for her help in making this book be the best book it could be!

Thank you to my sister, Kizzy. I found writing this book, as it's so deeply personal, extremely difficult. I shared many tears while writing it. Revisiting painful memories is no fun, but I knew I had to. Kiz was always there, picking up my calls, exchanging stories about Mum and telling me how proud she was of me. I couldn't ask for a better big sister.

My best friend, Charlie Craggs. In the final weeks of finishing this book, she was living with me and I must have been such a pain in the butt, constantly running into the living room spewing ideas at her while she tried to watch TV. But she always stopped the programme and listened. And she always told me how clever I was. I really needed that. Thank you, my ketchup queen.

And a massive thank you to all of these wonderful people who invested their precious time in helping take this book to the next level: Dr Kit Heyam, Kasey Robinson, Anick Soni and Nova Reid for helping to proofread. All the team at DK and Max Pedliham for making such a sick cover!

And lastly, I want to thank me. So often we give others praise, but when do we praise ourselves? There have been so many moments in my life when it would have been easier to give up, to stop believing in myself, to become small. But I'm stronger than anything that has ever happened to me. No matter the disadvantage or the hardship, I've always believed in myself and that takes heart.

I left school when I was fifteen. My mum had cancer and it was clear my school was trying to kick me out because I was trans. I've struggled with spelling and grammar my whole life because of that missed education. But one day, I got asked to write an article. I found it challenging. I believed I was a great storyteller, but I didn't have the skill set of a great writer. I wrote another article and I got slightly better. I asked others to help me and I got slightly better. Three years later, I got this, my first book deal.

Look at me now. Never stop believing in yourself.